The Cost of Forgiveness

Sandra J. Loman

TEACH Services, Inc.
P U B L I S H I N G
www.TEACHServices.com • (800) 367-1844

World rights reserved. This book or any portion thereof may not be copied or reproduced in any form or manner whatever, except as provided by law, without the written permission of the publisher, except by a reviewer who may quote brief passages in a review.

The author assumes full responsibility for the accuracy of all facts and quotations as cited in this book. The opinions expressed in this book are the author's personal views and interpretations, and do not necessarily reflect those of the publisher.

This book is provided with the understanding that the publisher is not engaged in giving spiritual, legal, medical, or other professional advice. If authoritative advice is needed, the reader should seek the counsel of a competent professional.

Copyright © 2022 Sandra J. Loman
Copyright © 2022 TEACH Services, Inc.
ISBN-13: 978-1-4796-1518-6 (Paperback)
ISBN-13: 978-1-4796-1519-3 (ePub)
Library of Congress Control Number: 2022906227

Published by

Table of Contents

Prologue . . . .*v*

Chapter 1   The Library 7

Chapter 2   The Art Store 10

Chapter 3   Home. 14

Chapter 4   Encounter on the Trail 19

Chapter 5   The Website 27

Chapter 6   Jefferson 32

Chapter 7   A Small-Town Church. 40

Chapter 8   Bible Words 46

Chapter 9   The Fisher Family. 52

Chapter 10   Nicole 58

Chapter 11	The Grocery Store	62
Chapter 12	Jefferson's Computer	67
Chapter 13	Confrontation	76
Chapter 14	Ellen	85
Chapter 15	Hallway Photos	93
Chapter 16	Friendship	95
Chapter 17	Lee, Andy, and Eliana	102
Chapter 18	Books	108
Chapter 19	Confessions	114
Chapter 20	The Letter	127
Chapter 21	Ethan	139
Chapter 22	The Fisher Family and Nicole	146
Chapter 23	Nathan and Nicole	152
Chapter 24	Nathan	159
Chapter 25	Forgiveness	166

Prologue

With snow crutching under my boots, I picked my way up the hiking trail located in the forest behind my home. The winter sun peeked through the canopy of trees, delivering pockets of warmth in the middle of an ocean of cold, but refusing to offer more before the advent of spring.

Of course, I had picked the chilliest day to venture out for some exercise, but I was pretty sure that my physical therapist didn't intend for me to tread through snow.

But, oh, this was so much more fun than a treadmill!

My frozen features felt as if they were cracking as a smile appeared on my face. No matter how many times I had walked on that machine, the scenery never changed; nothing could match the feeling of the woods with its contrasting stillness and life. Reaching out my hand, I bushed dew drops off a leaf, the dampness sinking into my gloved fingers.

Keeping my breathing shallow to avoid cold air in my lungs, I fought the urge to challenge myself by speeding up the incline to where the trail wound by a cliff overlooking the forest. A slight bend in the trail concealed anyone who might be approaching from down the hill, and that explained how a hiker appeared with warning.

The male figure on the trail, clothed in a black shirt and cargo pants, caused a sense of wariness in me; this was in contrast to the isolated but safe feeling I had enjoyed moments earlier that was now mixed with a fear of this stranger. The brim of his baseball hat was pulled down, and his masked face increased my sense of caution. When we passed each other, he glanced up at me.

Suddenly, my world turned gray, mocking the crisp green of the trees.

His face, flushed by the chilly air, had aged, lines appearing around the eyes, but that diamond-shaped jawline had stayed firm. The long, straight nose did not stand out, but his oval-shaped eyes, gray with a glint of blue, did.

The last time I had seen him, he had worn a haggard expression that would have broken hearts that didn't know the depths of his sins.

I last had seen him laughing, years ago but, of course, that mirth had faded.

No, actually the last time I had seen him, he had worn a haggard expression that would have broken hearts that didn't know the depths of his sins.

Was he sad? I wanted him to be sad. In that brief moment as our eyes locked, I searched for any sign of dejection and shame. Annoyance appeared instead, and he looked away with a scowl.

I moved past with measured steps, a new burden on my shoulders. Or rather, a burden carried for so long, now making itself felt.

CHAPTER 1

The Library

How do you forgive someone who has injured not only you, but the one you loved? Or, how do you move on from someone betraying you? Flowery words spoken from solemn faces paint forgiveness in glowing terms. The words say, 'forgiving makes you happier. It releases burdens. You may struggle with forgiving, but true Christians embrace forgiveness, because God forgave them.'

Few speak or even understand about the dark nights, the haunted thoughts, or the pain of betrayal you bear. You want to let go, you want to move on, but your wounds still bleed. Hurting and twisted up inside, you beg God to be able to forgive. You want to forget and, for a time, you do, but it all comes back—the betrayal or betrayals. You withdraw from people because they might hurt you, and you could hurt them.

—ReesesCup76, The Cost of Forgiveness Blog

I scanned the words that I had typed on the screen. So dramatic! Will my followers see this post as being overboard?

No wonder we trip and fall, when we keep looking backwards.

I finished the blog post and closed my laptop. Dim light streamed from the windows, heralding a chill awaiting me outside the building. My fellow library patrons, many of whom existed in their own mental rooms, appeared unaware of my inspection. Of those within my sphere of vision, most either sat at tables, as I had, or walked around perusing books. With my back toward the windows, the bookshelves blocked my view of the private study rooms separating the children's section from the adult's area. Instead, I turned to watch the people hunched in front of the computer screens to the left of the shelves. The circulation desk sat just beyond them, with its crew of librarians always clicking on their computers. They never appeared bored, having perfected the air of distracted professors interrupted by students, although the students were their patrons.

Now, feeling calmer after the brief respite of observing, I picked up my laptop and slipped it into my computer bag. Gathering my notebook and pen, I put them away as well. As I stood up and shouldered my bag, pain shot through my legs and back, protesting my movement, the muscles tight after an hour of sitting still. With a wince, I stretched as much as possible, while fighting the urge to yawn. Why does sleep beckon during the day but flee at night, I wondered?

Gritting my teeth, I hobbled over to the nonfiction section, my left thigh threatening rebellion against movement. Pacing gingerly up and down the rows until my muscles warmed to action, I halted at last in front of the Religion section. So many beliefs and, within the Christianity subsection, so many theories. This library provided a decent number of theology books that discussed and debated the various books of the Bible as well as the various Christian saints and biblical scholars. Books by modern-day evangelists proclaimed their ideas of what God wants and how to be happy.

Well, I wanted to be happy.

Moving my finger over some of the familiar titles, I searched for an unread book dealing with forgiveness and regret. Funny how most of those books resided, not in the Religion section, but in the Self-help section. Forgiveness and God go hand in hand, except in the library classification system. "Forgiveness is something you do for yourself"—I'd heard that proclaimed time and again. "You are not injuring the betrayer by withholding forgiveness from yourself; instead, you create your own mortal wound."

Well, not mortal. I've been bleeding for years, but I'm still standing. With that thought, I made my way out of the library, smiling in passing at a few familiar faces. The chilly air kissed my skin once I was outside because the clouds were being selfish with the sky. Deceived by the earlier sunlight, I had left my jacket in the truck. Picking up my pace—my long hair shielding me from the drizzle of rain against the back of my neck and my skin prickled up in bumps—I hurried to a place of warmth as the truck responded to the key remote in my hand. I opened the passenger side door of my truck and tossed my bag in before going around and getting inside. Once I inserted the key into the ignition, I leaned back, resting my head against the seat, staring at the library as I waited for the truck to warm up.

The stone walls of the library glistened from the increasing rain, but the rain marred the large glass windows, bringing a sense of dreariness to their otherwise attractive appearance. A structure, called the Story Silo, was attached to the side of the main building, resembling a protective tower by a castle.

While researching the small West Virginian town where I lived, I discovered that the grant funding the new library's construction had required an eco-friendly design. With all the signs inside the building, one became well informed that 100% recycled materials had been used to construct the Story Silo, and it had been built from sustainably grown wood, as well as materials from the previous library building. Large oval windows, strategically placed, provided natural light that reduced the need for artificial lights. Sleeping trees and bushes dotted the landscape, with the cheerful green of the evergreens beckoning from the surrounding park.

I spent more time there than anywhere else, enough to have a nodding acquaintance with a few of the regulars; but, outside of hellos or passing comments on books or library events, I kept to myself. Maybe the rainy weather was aiding my depression, and, at times, I wished I shared my brother's outgoing personality. A smile touched my lips as I thought of him. Jeremy would have scolded me for that thought, even if my parents agreed with me.

With warm air blowing loudly out of the vent, I buckled my seat belt and backed out of the parking spot, my thoughts drifting to Jeremy, Mom, and Dad.

CHAPTER 2

The Art Store

The inability to forgive and forget has become an obsession with me. A Christian who cannot forgive isn't a Christian at all, or so many claim. I believe in God, but I cannot forget. Train up a child, the Bible says, and when he is old, he will not depart from it. Here I am, far from the gracious nature my parents strove to instill. The nature they both possessed that passed me over. Even their professions testified to their caring natures.

My father was a minster, my mother, a nurse. A normal combination in our denomination, as was the number of children they had. A respectable two, one of each gender. My parents were the perfect representatives of respectable.

Dad was tall, handsome, and, by the time I knew him, had thick, white hair. He wore short-sleeve, button-down shirts and tan slacks whenever he could, even in the winter. Mom used to laugh at his outfit, sometimes buying him T-shirts and cargo shorts that were popular at one point. Dad wore those a few times, then put them away. Each time he returned to his old clothes, Mom would shake her head, smiling. In time, she donated the clothes she had bought.

Mom, even now I see her mass of graying curls from a perm, her petite frame, and serene brown eyes. She performed each of her roles in life efficiently—nurse, pastor's wife, and mother. In addition, she served as friend and, for some, a lifeline they could hold on to. There were times when Dad ended up finishing the dinner Mom had started because a church member or friend needed her. In all fairness, Mom played the fill-in for Dad as well. Something about my parents encouraged people to lean on them, to feel comforted by their presence. They weren't perfect—as a teenager I can attest to their rather strict nature. The same face that wore a charming smile for his congregation could turn to stone as Dad reprimanded me for my choice of music. Mom's cheery voice could become shrill as she warned me about the clothing I wore. Looking back, I could see them being tired, having had a child when most already had grandchildren. Years of infertility preceded my brother's birth. More barren years followed, then my own birth.

—ReesesCup76, The Cost of Forgiveness Blog

How many times did I attempt to sneak out of the house at night to breathe in the night air and see the stars in all their glory, only to find Dad waiting at the foot of the stairs. It didn't help that their bedroom, a converted office, was on the main floor, while Jeremy's and mine were on the second story. My bedroom, the old primary bedroom, was located above my parents' bedroom and, in that old house, floors creaked. For a while, Dad always heard my approach as I came down the stairs. No climbing out the window either, unless I wanted to jump. In fact, I tried to jump out of my window just once. Only ten years of age when we moved to that house, I tested my limits. I snickered to myself as I drove through town, remembering how I jumped out of the window. I positioned our trampoline where I thought I would land. My miscalculations resulted in a broken foot and arm!

Maybe my parents' gray hair appeared after I was born, I mused, as I navigated the downtown roads, looking for a parking spot in the back-alley parking lots. Mouth twisted in a frown, I gave up and parallel parked on the street, taking up two spots. At least I won't have trouble getting out. Well, that's if the cars in front and behind me don't move.

Jeremy sold the house after Mom and Dad died.

My shoulders sagged at the memory. I shut the truck door and locked it with a press of the button. Crossing the street, jacket pulled tightly around me, I almost ran down the deserted sidewalk to the small art store. Inside a small crowd wandered around, waiting perhaps for the rain to slow.

Seeing no one I knew, but not surprised, I kept my head down and rushed through my shopping. No one spoke to me, outside of mumbled excuses. And this is what I reproved myself for just a short time ago. I sighed. Heading to the front of the store to the line gathered there, I smiled at the other people around. At the front of the line, polite smile still fixed in place, I confronted the young female sales clerk with an inquiry on her wellness.

Safe subject, right?

"Doing alright," she answered, "you?"

Before I could reply, she continued.

"Dad's loving the crowd today."

"Oh?"

"He owns the store. I'm just a temp, helping out during my break—whether I want to or not," she added under her breath. She flushed. She said her name was April.

I chuckled, "What school do you attend?"

She named a familiar college, and we chatted about it as she bagged my purchases.

With a friendly smile, April wished me a good day as I exited the shop.

Years ago, my social circle was larger and involved face-to-face conversations, more than the texting and e-mailing my social life consisted of now. Why did this little interaction lighten my spirits? Perhaps I was emerging from my mental isolation. Reminding myself that chatting with April wasn't really socializing, I still hummed a melody as I returned to my truck.

"Nice parking job."

Teeth aching from the sudden clenching, I placed my purchases in the truck and shut the passenger door before turning around. A tall man wearing a light brown jacket and blue jeans grinned at me. My nearest neighbor, the one who shared my driveway.

Why is he talking to me? The day had gone so well; I had even made small talk, and now, here he was. How fast the world had gone downhill.

He shifted on his feet, his smile slipping as I stared at him.

"You are almost out on the road." He gestured with a nod of his head to the distance between my truck and the curb, a good foot apart.

"Yeah, I hate parallel parking," my voice flat. I crossed my arms.

His dim smile looking uncertain, but he still teased, "It shows. How are you doing neighbor? Haven't seen you around."

He sounded so well, friendly. Local gossip informed me this neighbor avoided company. All the times I'd encountered him before had occurred while hiking. I had received a curt nod or, at most, a brief "Hello." I assumed he was as eager to return to solitude as I was. Despite that, he stood there, in the middle of town, attempting to make conversation.

Perhaps the upcoming holiday had made him friendlier, or it was possible he felt isolation weighing heavily on him today, as I had. Maybe I should have stopped making assumptions and just talked. He looked nervous now.

Wondering why I should care about his discomfort, I summoned a passably pleasant tone.

"Lots of work, not a lot of time for hikes, unfortunately."

"I've been busy as well. Finally run of food, I'm here to restock."

"Did I…." I bit the words off, my cheeks flushed. "I mean, I should go. Nice seeing you."

His gunmetal-colored eyes—why do I always notice eyes—widened from my slip, and he muttered "Uh, yeah, bye."

I escaped into my truck. With a glance in my rear-view mirror, I pulled out and onto the road. He stood there, watching me drive away.

CHAPTER 3

Home

By the time I turned twelve, I learned to avoid the creaks in the stairs, managing to sneak out at night. Not to meet friends or make trouble, but to wander the empty streets. We lived where you could see the stars, even in town. I would walk with my face up, staring at the sprinkling of lights. Walking in the quiet of the night, acquainted with the night, as Robert Frost once wrote. How I identified with that poem the day I found it among the poems Mom assigned for me to read. I analyzed the poem and wrote a paper on it for English class, exploring the various analyses of the poem. Many suggested the poem spoke of depression: the loneliness of the man walking alone late at night, how he failed to connect to the watchman passing by, not wanting to explain. His cry and the lack of caring expressed by no one calling back or saying good-bye. No one cared.

I felt that loneliness in my own soul, but I didn't feel depressed. Not yet. I wandered the night to avoid thinking, but all that ended the night I attempted to sneak back inside and met my father returning from the kitchen with a glass of water. Only twelve, I could not understand his fear upon discovering what I had been doing. As an adult, I understand it too well.

Chapter 3: Home

> *Nighttime, after that, represented prison. Dad, my guard, shutting off access to the outside.*
>
> *Dad never understood why I felt the need to wander at night. Sometimes I caught him watching me, his brows knitted, his lips pulled tight. Every time my eyes met his, his face softened, and he would give me a small smile. Mom worried also, with words. She would press me, every so often , to talk to her. Funny how so many confided in my parents, but I felt uncomfortable doing so.*
>
> —ReesesCup76, The Cost of Forgiveness Blog

Eager to escape my neighbor, I later questioned my rudeness. Would it have hurt me to engage in conversation? Ignoring the whispers that it might have, I decided to be more polite next time. If he was friendly still, of course. If not, no worries.

As I mused over safe topics of conversation, the street sign signaling my turn off had almost sped past me. Jerking the steering wheel to the right, the truck lurched forward as it left the pavement. I turned the wipers on to clear the mud sprays on the windshield. Perhaps the neighborhood could look into putting down gravel on the road or at least smoothing out the ridges that challenged my suspension.

Open fields gave way to trees as I slowed my speed, conscious of occasional horse riders and hikers traveling to where the road dead-ended in the state forest. Sometimes lost hikers cut across my three-acre property where one hiking trail ended. An acceptable annoyance in exchange for obtaining one of the most sought-after locations in the area, limited in available houses due to the forest conservation laws that prevented new development. I paid heavily for that privilege.

Worth it.

I thought seeing a house and knowing it was your home was a romantic, but unrealistic, notion. Like love at first sight. Wrong twice. That love was a heartbreak ago, but I knew this house was home the moment I pulled into the driveway behind the agent.

Turning off the road into my gravel driveway, I saw the small split-level home, perched on a hill, peeking out from the trees. Following the curve to the left where the road divided, the truck rolled down the slope, stopping in front of the garage door. Turning off the engine, I gathered my things before opening the truck door....

And fell on my side, hip hitting the ground, one hand trying to halt my fall.

Okay, so maybe I shouldn't have grabbed everything in one go. Great. Laptop, okay? Yep. Paints, perfectly shaken.

Leaving the bags on the ground, I maneuvered myself to a standing position. Checking over my hands and clothes before retrieving my bags, I felt my face grow uncomfortably warm. Wasn't like anyone saw, though.

Ascending the stairs leading to the sidewalk, palm stinging, I moseyed up the walk to the front porch. After shuffling around the bags, I unlocked the door.

Dim light filtered inside from the windows on either side and above the door, illuminating the small foyer enough for my eyes to adjust. Perhaps I should have left the original windowpane door, as this one only had one small pane of glass toward the top. My eyes adjusted; I paused to kick off my shoes before crossing the stone-floor landing to the stairs to the right that led to the living area. Passing through the family room, depressingly dark with the curtains drawn over the large windows, I walked through to the dining area.

Coldness prickled my skin. Maybe a fire would help heat the area. I frowned, looking into the room just beyond the dining area, where a small wood-burning stove sat on a hand-laid stone platform.

Depositing my things on the wooden table, I entered the back room and checked the wood box. Empty. Massaging the soreness growing in my hip with one hand, I opened the sliding glass door to the left, stepping onto the deck. Two trips to the tarp-protected wood pile next to the deck, one short rest to retrieve pain medicine from the kitchen cabinet, and I began savoring the warmth starting filled the area.

Satisfied with the fire, I hobbled over to the kitchen for a glass of water. Grabbing a glass that that still smelled of stain from when I had stripped and refinished the kitchen cabinets, I filled the glass with water from the kitchen faucet. Sipping the cool liquid, I glazed out the window over the sink to the tree line beyond the deck.

Beyond the trees sat my neighbor's home, the one who shared my driveway. Rumor was, the grove of trees had been planted a century ago by feuding neighbors; now, it extended the state forest. Given the large amount of trees and their various sizes, I doubted the gossip. The original house on my side had long ago been torn down; the current one where I lived had been built in 1976. My neighbor's house was apparently sturdier and had been treated more kindly. The original house still stood, but with some additions.

So I looked up the local houses on a real estate site. Curiosity isn't the same as nosiness. It isn't.

Washing out my glass, I set it to dry on the counter. Time to change clothes, as the damp fabric chafed my skin. Grabbing the laptop bag, I retrieved the art supplies as well. Warmth at my back, I reentered the living, turning right to the long hallway ending in my bedroom. Ducking through the door to my office on the right side of the hallway, I dropped the bags on the floor, freeing my laptop. The rain present a few seconds ago pelted now against the window over the large desk. With a sigh, I plugged my computer into the charging cable. I went to the large closet, from which I had removed the closet doors. Organizational bins filled this space, and I sorted out the paints, brushes, and tools I had purchased.

Stretching, I gazed around the room, debating what to start on. Oh, right, clothes. Exiting the room, I entered my bedroom. Why did I insist on wearing these fancy clothes? I mean, really, did I really expect to meet a prospective client wandering around the library bookshelves? In the art shop?

So I looked up the local houses on a real estate site. Curiosity isn't the same as nosiness. It isn't.

Trying to remember the last time I had designed a website for a small business, I balanced on alternating legs as I pulled off the thin dress socks. Snugging my feet into the lush carpet of the bedroom—dark green to complement the sage color of the walls—I was grateful I had installed carpeting instead of continuing the stone-and-wood flooring of the rest of the house. I went into the walk-in closet where the dresser sat against the back wall. Retrieving worn jeans from the drawer and a long-sleeve thermal shirt from the hangers, I exited the closet and laid the clothes on the king-sized bed. As I discarded the blouse and slacks in the hamper by my on-suite bathroom, my palm began stringing again, and I discovered a bruise starting to form on my hip as well.

Gritting my teeth, I dressed before cleaning off my palm and rubbing ointment on it. Stomach growling, I realized I had forgotten to grab lunch while in town. Why? Oh, yeah, the neighbor. Remembering the spark of interest in his eyes, I rubbed my fingers between my eyes. Maybe I had imagined it. Maybe kittens fly, too, with cute little golden wings.

If he only knew how I despised him….

I shook my head, heading to the kitchen.

CHAPTER 4

Encounter on the Trail

Are some people predisposed to forgive easily? Shall we analyze my childhood, readers? A warning first. It's not a riveting tale.

Still there? Good. Here we go.

My personality didn't mesh well with other children, as proven by my brief stay at our small church school. A stage took up the back wall of the gymnasium and, during playtime while the other children ran around the gym during the rainy days, I sat on the stage side stairs, observing. My teacher mistakenly thought I was shy and encouraged me to join the others during free play. I did, for a short time, before retreating back to my position on the stairs. I preferred watching. In fairness to myself, I should rephrase my earlier statement. I meshed well with other children for limited amounts of time. That said, once I had withdrawn for a while, I wanted acceptance when I returned. Children do not work like that;, remove yourself from a circle long enough, and the circle will close the gap. I learned to take part in play or risk being left out.

> *Funny how much I resented that. When the school closed down and Mom started homeschooling me, there was relief from not pretending anymore. It didn't take long for me to discover that. Certain things were expected of the pastor's daughter. Out of control or a little saint, but not much middle ground. The middle ground was where I wanted to fit in, but others tried to push me to either end.*
>
> *Was this when I became unforgiving? Was it when others ignored who I was in favor of who they projected me to be? They put me in a box and set me aside, forgetting I could climb out. While my parents struggled with a balance between supporting me and encouraging me to present a Christian appearance, Jeremy became my lifeline. How many e-mails and letters I wrote to him, pouring out my thoughts and troubles.*
>
> —ReesesCup76, The Cost of Forgiving Blog

The drizzle of rain became a prophet to herald the arrival of a storm. With the rapid decline in temperance, a mix of ice and rain pelted me when I moved my truck into the garage.

At least I have no dog to walk. Not yet.

Contemplating the quiet stillness of the house interior versus the rage of water outside, I thought perhaps I should adopt a ferret instead. It would quickly undo the work I'd done to the house, but those updates and repairs had come from needing physical labor to relax my mind. Even more work might be good, giving me more to do; outsmarting a ferret determined to find all the nooks and crannies would keep my mind busy.

I smirked, maybe a cat instead. We can pace the hallway at night together. A Christmas present to myself? I wondered if there was a black Friday sale today on cat items? Not that I was thinking about heading back into town.

Friday passed. I remembered how I wished as a child to be left alone. Well, I'm alone now. It had been nine months since I moved away from normality and reminders, memories packing themselves in the moving truck as I fled. Saturday gave no respite, although I disappeared into Bible study, researching forgiveness for the blog.

Saturday evening, relief came in the form of a heads-up text regarding a new advertising campaign. During the next twenty-four odd hours, from sunset Saturday to late Sunday night, I worked on the campaign, setting up websites, registering new domain names, and creating ads to submit to the advertising companies to distribute. After catching up on sleep—nothing like exhausting yourself to keep restlessness at bay—and eating, I went out onto the deck.

Damp air kissed my drowsy senses, and I wrapped the wool jacket more tightly around me. The action kicked up the ghost of the original owner's smell. Hugging myself, the deck rail wetting my coat sleeves as I leaned forward, I inspected the yard and woods beyond. The flashes of light as the sunlight touched water drops on the grass brought a smile to my lips. The sun still found ways to lighten the gray world.

From the deck, I spotted the path leading into the grove of trees. Mentally, I walked the path to where it joined the established state park trail, hilly, and rather fun to navigate. No lost adventurers there for a few days at least, unless the trail escaped the fate of mud and ice.

Hmm. I should try the hike, if only because the ache in my legs protested the sedentary days. Well, my choice: use the treadmill downstairs or chance the slippery path?

Path. Mud's fun. Now where did I put my hiking boots?

Exchanging the jacket for a lightweight water-resistant coat in preparation for the coming exertion and chance of more rain, I laced up the boots and grabbed the house key. Back door locked, I walked down the deck stairs to the open area of the back yard. Passing the fire pit and then the once-nice garden left to weeds because of cold weather and my lazy habits, my body turned against me, furious at the exercise. I can't win. Rest or move, my body hates me.

Forcing a brisk pace, I entered the forest line, following the path until it met the official state trail. On the other side, the path continued, eventually ending at the neighbor's property. No marks on the path from what I saw, good. Turning left onto the path, my foot slide sideways. Catching myself, I slowed my pace to start ascending the hilly terrain.

The hem of my jeans grew muddy, as my mind cleared in the fresh air. A different quiet from the house, here in the forest where the trees and creatures slept. Now, evergreens cheerily bragged their wakeful state, with an occasional winter bird scolding the chill of the air. Sleep meant they could wake again, and nothing dead save leaves and fallen tree limbs, both of which broke down to feed new life.

The words of Longfellow's poem, "Woods in Winter,"[1] came to my lips, breaking the living quiet. My voice faded as I confronted a tree lying across the trail.

"You are ruining the moment," I mumbled, puffing as I tried to climb over its thick trunk. The soreness in my side protested, with my leg joining in, and I gave in to the mutiny, retracing my steps down the trail.

I wondered again at how rarely I encountered the neighbors sharing this trail, despite it winding past their backyards. Well, neither did any of them ever knock on my door. The realtor selling my house assured me that everyone here enjoyed their privacy. In fact, most tended toward retirement age and were a tight group, sharing a bond of descending from the original settlers of the area. They were less than interested in new neighbors, she implied, especially the person who had brought the house after their long-time neighbor had died. Perhaps that reminded them of their own ages.

I shook my head involuntary at that thought, which had come from one of the few neighbors to reach out to me, Ellen. Aged herself, with a wrinkled face and thin frame, Ellen delivered both information and gossip in a matter-of-fact tone. She was the one, in fact, who talked about Jefferson. Another descendant of original settlers, he had inherited the house from his grandparents five years ago.

"Such a sweet little boy, always coming over for a visit and a cookie. His grandparents, Mae and Paul, they were so proud of him becoming a photographer and making a good living at it, too. Mae always loved taking pictures, you know; she spent hours showing that child the ins and outs of the darkroom. At the end, now, they worried." Ellen's lips pursed, "Still single, and Mae hinted that his heart had been broken." Ellen shook her head.

"Well, I'm single. It's not too bad." I smiled at her.

"Don't get ideas about Jefferson. I know the mysterious air appeals to some women, but I don't want you hurt. He shouldn't be alone now; his grandparents wouldn't want that. But there are other young men around here. I could introduce you to them," she added with a coy smile.

I barked a laugh at the memory. That had been the first day of knowing Ellen, and she tried to fix me up with one of her church friends' sons. Certain personalities astound me. Is being single that offensive? It took

---

[1] Longfellow, Henry W. "Woods in Winter." 1890. Public domain.

six months for Ellen to take a hint and stop pushing me to meet someone. More than a hint, I flat out told her if I wanted male company, some male friends had expressed interest, despite my lack of such. Being mobile themselves, the distance between us didn't seem to bother them. Besides, choosing someone nearby and sharing acquaintances, made it awkward when it ended.

"Oh sweetie, why would it need to end?" Ellen inquired.

I shrugged, "Most things do, but I'm too exhausted currently to deal with relationships."

Both physically and emotionally, but I did not share that. I couldn't go through that again. Another reason to avoid dating—feelings get involved. The fire of passion warms lonely nights, but one gets burned.

Meeting my firm refusal to consider dating, Ellen surprised me by halting her pushiness.

However, Ellen never stopped trying to pry my story out of me, wanting to open me up and examine me. Unbidden, a smile grew on my face, as I saw her twinkling eyes as she dropped a question here and there, always with an innocent air.

At least such personalities made for good characters in my stories, not that I ever walked the two miles to her home to gather material for character development.

I rolled my shoulders. Soon after meeting Ellen, I had encountered Jefferson on the trail. That cold day, when my world was regaining light, turned dim again.

Someone had a sense of humor or perhaps was testing me, because Jefferson and I encountered each other regularly on the trail. I altered my hiking times—going early morning or late evening—but it appeared he did the same, unfortunately. I finally set no schedule, going at random times. That appeared to work; our encounters happening less often. Each encounter, after the first, went the same way. No words exchanged, maybe a nod of acknowledgment, and no more eye contact. Two wanderers passing each other by, wrapped in armor of isolation. Poetic, if each encounter hadn't brought pain.

With relief, I spotted my little side path, almost forgetting to go slowly on the descent in my eagerness to flee my thoughts. Intent on my path, I failed to notice my surroundings.

"Reisa."

Blowing out a long breath, I turned, facing Jefferson.

"Hello," I fixed my features into a friendly smile. Remembering my rudeness last Friday, I added in an apologetic tone, "I'm sorry I rushed off last time we met."

Jefferson scanned my face, his hands in his coat pockets, apparently waiting for me to say more.

My smile faltered slightly. "Okay, well, good-bye." I will not hand out lame excuses about why I rushed off.

"It's all good," he said before I could turn away. "Did you have a bit of trouble on the trail?"

I follow his gaze to my dirty hands and clothes. "Yeah, a tree fell over, blocking the trail. I attempted to climb over. Didn't work well for me." I shrugged.

"Aye, I'll tell the park rangers about it," he said, withdrawing his hands from his coat.

"I should have that number," I frowned. "I never thought to look it up."

"I'll call them," he repeated. "Your leg okay? I saw you limping."

Here I thought I had lurched along unnoticed.

"Yep. Old war injury." I flashed a smile, "Or maybe it came from when I wrestled that angel."

"Your name Jacob?" he quizzed, his eyes twinkling.

"You know your Bible."

"Surprisingly, yes." He didn't appear offended by my surprise.

"Well, I'll hobble along to my tents. I have a robe to work on."

"You're not very social, are you?"

I felt my smile fade, "No, not really, Growing up around sheep can make you a bit sheepish around strangers."

A chuckle burst out of him, "Okay, that was lame. Did Jacob grow up around sheep? Never mind; of course he did."

"Well, good-bye," I said cheerfully, heading down the path away from Jefferson. The sound of footsteps behind me told me I hadn't shaken him loose yet. I ignored him until I reach the clearing near the garden.

Why can't he go away?

Why didn't I move once I saw him? Oh yeah, demons like to give chase. Didn't they follow me to West Virginia, and increase. This was definitely an increase. Instead of the peace I sought, here was a living reminder of how I failed to forgive.

Yeah, I need to post later on the forgiveness blog; maybe some commenter can suggest how I can handle this. Strange man follows me to my house, haunting my steps both literally and figuratively. Turn around, coward.

Wordlessly I faced Jefferson, waiting for his explanation as to why he was following me.

An embarrassed, boyish look crept over his face. Really, he seemed too old to pull off that look.

"It occurred to me that over the months you have lived here, I haven't been neighborly."

"Hmm. Well, bake me a cake or some cookies, and we'll call it square."

Still I waited, his rigid stance suggested more.

"Look, I need a website designer." He rubbed his jaw, looking away before returning his eyes to my face, "Ellen mentioned you are one." He bowed his head, still looking at me.

Business. I can handle business, but should I?

Chewing my lower lip while thinking about my schedule, I mumbled that I could manage a bit of time to work on a site, depending on what he wanted.

When out, I dressed nicely to impress possible clients, and now I landed one while wearing dirty jeans. Go figure.

Oh great, do I invite him in to discuss it? I glanced over my shoulder to my house, then back to him. He had given up the coy look, eying me with puzzlement.

Do I want him in my home?

Focus.

"What type of site are you looking for?" I asked.

"Business, somewhere to sell my photos. My current website, well, is awful."

"Who designed it?"

"I did," he admitted.

"Hmm. Well, I'm in the middle of a project currently, but I can squeeze in some time." I searched my coat for paper and pen, then my pockets. Nothing.

"Let me grab my business card and give you my e-mail address so you can send me a list of what you want."

"Well, I'm not totally sure what I want." He furrowed his brow, "Would you mind going over my website with me, maybe giving me some suggestions?"

The table and chairs on the deck were wet, or else I could have brought my laptop outside and worked with him there. Another deep breath, and I nodded.

Heavenly Father, you are really pushing me here.

"You have a minute? We can do it now."

"Yep," He replied.

I marched to the house, leaving him to follow.

CHAPTER 5

The Website

To those of you who complained that I sounded rather spoiled or perhaps needed therapy to deal with my antisocial nature, well, thanks for the input. I will give it the consideration such opinions/advice deserve.

No, this blog isn't becoming a memoir.

And yet we continue down the path through my past. Skip over this post if that doesn't appeal to you, but background, people, background is important! The past molds us, and childhood wounds can tear us apart as adults, etc., etc.

I forget, sometimes, how my parents knew me, even if they didn't understand me.

I homeschooled through high school, Mom choosing to politely ignore the suggestions and admonitions of various church members: support our academies, schools are closing due to a lack of students, and the pastor needs to set an example by sending his daughter.

I didn't want to go.

If my parents had been strict having one teenager, the school—having many teenagers—had been stricter still. In the nineties the rules governing female and male interactions were becoming dated, but still enforced.

Not that I actually cared about that.

No, it was the fact that I would have no privacy. At home, my parents had long ago accepted my need to disappear into my room for quiet. I doubted my roommates would. I knew kids attending the academy, seeing them on breaks and during the summer. They shared a wide spectrum of experiences in academy: some loved it, some hated it, and some were apathetic. In addition to having no privacy, seeing my parents rarely failed to appeal. Whether my parents discussed it, or if my mom never even considered the idea, I do not know. They only once asked me if I wanted to go, when I was fourteen. At my negative answer, the subject was never mentioned again. I finished high school with A's and had little trouble finding a college. I forget, sometimes, how my parents knew me, even if they didn't understand me.

—ReesesCup76, The Cost of Forgiving Blog

Love of money is the root of evil. Not that I love money, but I like to work and keeping my name out there to bring in more business is important.

Which leads to some uncomfortable situations, apparently, for here's Jefferson, sitting at my dining room table, using my laptop to bring up his website.

I shifted on my feet, rubbing one arm, his slow typing needling my nerves.

"Here you go," Jefferson said, getting out of the chair. I slid in, focusing on the site, not on how he squatted down next to me, his head near my own.

The word *annoyed* fit my emotions. Personal space is not a new concept; they should teach it in schools.

"Is your issue with lack of traffic to your site or are you having issues with web interface?"

"Yes." He groaned.

Fighting a smile now along with annoyance, I assured him, "I can help with both."

I clicked on his portfolio and scrolled through the photos. Hmm, fine arts photography, surprising. Rather good, and familiar, too. I'd seen that photo of a cat in the rain before. Clicking on the "About" tab informed me that Jefferson Fisher had a degree in photography and worked for several reputable magazines. I moved my chair back after a few more moments, and he stood in response. Turning in the chair to gaze up at him, I realized our close proximity. I stood instead. With the chair between us, I indicated the computer with a wave of my hand.

"I can redesign the site to be more attractive to customers, functional, and responsive. However, you need your own domain name. From what I have read, you are already established in the photography world, and I've seen your stuff before. Awesome work, but you need your site to reflect that. I can set up the site for you to maintain yourself, if you want or, for a small fee, I can maintain it for you."

He crossed his arms, "I would rather maintain it."

I nodded my head, "No problem. I can make that work. I need to get back to my other work, but why don't we set up a time to go over things? Okay?," I bent over my laptop, opening some tabs and typing in URLs. I stepped back, nodding toward the screen, "Here's some of the websites I've designed."

I stepped back as he moved over to look, glancing over to the kitchen. Should I offer him a drink? Of course, manners.

"Wow, I'm impressed." He straightened up, "Honestly."

Jefferson sounded a bit surprised. I looked back just in time to see him bend back down as he scrolled down to the bottom of the site where my name was.

"Jensen, huh. Ellen never mention your last name."

"Yet she told you I designed websites." I closed the laptop, "I'll grab my business card."

I returned from my office, card in hand, to find him standing in my living room.

"I like the wooden beams on the ceiling." He looked up and then returned his gaze to me. "Cabin like."

"They were one of the features that sold me on this house."

He nodded, glancing around, "Did you change anything?"

"Never been inside before?"

"No, I didn't know the Dennisons well."

I held out my card. He took it and slid it in his pocket.

"I didn't change much. The wall color, of course, the beige before was boring. I changed the flooring in the entryway to stone, Added carpet to the primary bedroom. I redid the kitchen cabinets, updated the appliances. In the basement I...," I laughed softly. "I guess I changed more than I thought. Still, the heart of the house remained the same."

His face sharpened.

"The heart of the house," Jefferson repeated.

"Something my brother used to say. He had a poet's soul." I hugged myself, disquieted. Why did I mention Jeremy?

Jefferson noticed my action, opened his mouth, then apparently changed his mind on commenting. Walking over to the railing overlooking the foyer, he peered down.

"Why natural stone instead of ceramic? Ceramic tiles are more durable."

Frowning, what a question!.

I explained, "Depending on the type, of course. A salesperson attempted to talk me into the glazed tiles that resemble stone, but I preferred the look of travertine. No two stones are alike," I dropped my arms, "I do need to get back to work. If you want to e-mail me...."

Jefferson pulled out my card, glancing down at it.

"I prefer texting, do you have your cell number on here?" He flipped it over to look at the other side. "Do you have a cell?"

"I do, and, yes, it's listed on there. If that's all?" I walked to the back door, Jefferson trailing behind. Taking his coat off the coat hook by the door, I handed it to him. He took it, shrugging it on, a faint smile on his lips.

"You know, if you wanted me to leave, you do not have to be shy about it."

Cheeks reddening, I joked, "I know, I'm not assertive."

Opening the door, I added, "Hike safely now."

"I will," the smile remained on his lips, "I'll be in touch."

He stepped through the door, and I shut it behind him. Going over to the kitchen window, I watched as he went down the deck steps and crossed my back yard.

Good graces, have I really signed myself up for more interactions? Rubbing my eyes with the palms of my hands, I mumbled, "Give me strength."

Don't turn down business unless for a valid reason. Are mine valid reasons? Maybe I should pass this job to another web designer. If I backed out, would it make him curious? Why? Would it draw his interest? Am I overanalyzing this?

Probably.

Long enough break; time to go back to work.

CHAPTER 6

Jefferson

Yes, dear readers, my mother made sure to deal with the socialization issue. I went on mission trips for the church and other social outreach activities. Mom even found other homeschoolers, some local, some pen pals (remember the old writing-letters days?!).

I endured it all, brave soldier, with a smile on my face, but rebellion in my heart. Well, somewhat: I do admit to enjoying the mission trips and writing to someone all the way across the world.

Still, college allowed me freedoms that academy wouldn't have. My roommates became friends, a surprise to all. I actually didn't mind them around. They both went on to have tragedies of their own—not mine to share—but that first year we all delighted in freedom, even if our actions were tame by secular college standards. That year was the last year I felt whole.

Watching the parents of my roommates, as well as those of other students, brought home to me how blessed I was with my parents. Dad rarely raised his voice, Mom lacked a passive-aggressive streak. We may have had differing viewpoints on certain subjects— I stubbornly believed myself right on certain beliefs—but it wasn't war at home. The different personalities and the fact that they were older parents may have caused me to feel left out in the cold at times, but they had tried more than I thought.

Close to Christmas break, my brother showed up on campus. Since he lived in California, close to where my parents had retired the previous year and I went to school in Michigan, his unexpected arrival caused apprehension.

My parents had been killed in a car accident. Accident, despite the fact that the other driver ran the red light and hit them. Jeremy couldn't bear to break the news over the phone. My life blurred after that. I had never felt grief before, never lost someone to death. I had observed grief in others, visiting dying church members with my father when he thought my young face would be a comfort. Never felt that connection, never felt this numbness.

Jeremy and his wife pulled me through the funeral, encouraging me to transfer to a college closer to them. I ended up at a secular college, graduating with a dual degree in computer science and English. I should have pursued a master's in web development, but life got in the way. So destructive. Life finds cracks in one's plans, widening them into gorges until you find yourself standing on a cliff far from where you planned to be.

Losing my parents—when I finally felt free to see them as more than my parents—that hurt. I had Jeremy, and I had his wife. We all grew closer from the loss. The betrayal that came was a splinter into the heart. The flesh would tear if you removed it.

Forgiveness may push the splinter out, but memories poison the attempts to let go. But who do I need to forgive? Not yet, not sharing that quite yet.

—ReesesCup76, The Cost of Forgiving Blog

Blink once, and a week had sped by.

Connecting my iPod to the Bluetooth speakers in the office, I listened as "Viva la vida" by Coldplay filled the air. Grabbing a blank canvas from the bin, I set it down on the work table. Brushes, gel medium, a few laser-printed, black-and-white photos I had taken, and paint joined the canvas. Rolling up my sleeves, I started working, my thoughts drifting.

No text from Jefferson, and I felt no need to remind him. After all, he didn't provide me with contact information, and who wants someone showing up at your house uninvited.

Never mind the lightness in my breathing as each day passed without contact, leaving me better able to focus on my work and hobby. The latter currently consisted of the forgiveness blog, and I worked hard to reply to the comments.

Why did I start this blog again? Why share my life with others, the events leading up to that life-changing tragedy, the second that changed the course of my life? The comments were interesting, but that was no surprise. I'd always found other people's lives fascinating. Feeling, sharing, their pain, their joy, or even their annoyance, and yet not engaging but rather observing.

> *I'd always found other people's lives fascinating. Feeling, sharing, their pain, their joy, or even their annoyance, and yet not engaging but rather observing.*

At one point in my life, I surrounded myself with friends or, more truthfully, acquaintances. Their pain hurt me, and their ability to move on impressed me. I loved them, but I lost the one who knew my soul.

I found another who knew my heart.

Now I stand, years away from the time of betrayal, hours away from where my heart had been broken again, alone once more.

Shaking my head, I focused on the canvas in front of me. Tearing up strips of paper, I coated the backs and pasted them onto the canvas. With this project it did not matter that I lacked Mom's drawing ability. Here I could even paste words to enhance the photos, play with textures, and just have fun.

Jeremy, after Mom gave up interesting me in art, taught me about photography, his favorite hobby. Again, a fail. I could not master the darkroom, and I hated waiting to see how the photos turned out. Then digital single-lens reflex cameras (DSLRs) became affordable, combining cameras firmly with computers in my mind, but Jeremy missed that.

I swallowed, standing up and stretching my back. I needed to take my camera with me again while I hiked. I needed more photos to work with.

I need to take Ellen a painting, as she had asked about seeing some of my work. No, wait, she isn't home; she went to see the grandkids in Maryland.

That's good because, with her social personality, I can't imagine how she deals with an empty house. Well, maybe by gossiping and interfering with the lives of single women.

I snorted.

If she was in Maryland, when did she tell Jefferson about me? From the way she made it sound, he never responded to her overtures of friendship, despite her friendship with his grandparents.

Guess they made up. My phone meowed, signaling a text message. I finished up the first layer on the canvas and left it to dry. Before checking my phone, I cleaned up in the hall bathroom.

Then, I headed into the kitchen to grab a soda. I took a gulp as I picked up my phone with my free hand. Swiping with my thumb, I tapped to bring up the new message. Selene promised me another photo of Eleni; that girl looks like her mother but the attitude, that's all Selene.

A week's time had made me naive. I groaned at the unknown number of the next message.

"Sorry about the delay; here are some possible times I could meet up…"

I noticed the first time was only two hours away.

"This is Jefferson Fisher BTW."

Yeah, I figured that out.

"My work load is heavier than I thought when I talked with you last. I can suggest another designer if you want?" I texted back using the voice command.

The reply came instantly.

"No."

I sniggered. Did he think life worked like that? You could say "No," and people listened? I started to reply when another text arrived.

"I looked over your work and talked with a few of your clients. Everyone sang your praises. Plus, you live next door, easier to harass you if something goes wrong."

I deleted my original reply and texted instead: "That's an even better reason for me to decline. I value my privacy and separating my work from personal time."

"We should discuss your fee."

My mouth dropped. I'm refusing, you idiot! Tempted to text as much, I instead typed: "Beth Robinson has worked with other photographers to create e-commerce sites. Mention my name and she won't give a discount, but it will bug her enough that you came to me first that she will work that much harder to prove she's better." I added Beth's e-mail and website information.

I waited a few minutes. When he didn't reply, I put the phone down and finished my soda. Throwing it into the recycling bin in the back room, I grabbed a jacket off the coat hook. Opening the deck door, I walked outside and then sat in the Adirondack chair. The chilly air stung my lungs after breathing the heated air of the house.

I crossed my arms and tucked my hands under my shoulders to protect them. I closed my eyes, enjoying the fresh air, welcoming the chill. The weather late in the year had stayed warmer than usual, but still colder than where I used to live. In Michigan, didn't I go without a coat at this temperature? Living in warmer climates must have thinned my blood, as well as age and injuries making me more susceptible to the cold.

I smirked.

"Rather cold to take a nap outside, isn't it?"

Drawing a deep breath, I opened my eyes. Jefferson hadn't quite cleared the stairs, standing near the middle.

Taking in his florid cheeks, I comment wryly, "You must have run here. It hasn't been that long since my last text."

He climbed the remaining stairs. "I was texting on the way."

"Texting while hiking? Shame on you." I untucked my hands, straighten up in my seat. "You could have tripped over a rock."

"I like to live dangerously."

Pulling a chair from the outside table, he straddled it, looking down at me.

"Why don't you want to work for me?" he blurted out.

"Why were you walking over here while suggesting we met two hours from now?"

We glared at each other for a moment before he conceded.

"Intuition. I suspected I might have to convince you."

"How did you know I was home?"

"Nope, my turn for an answer," he chided., "Why did you change your mind?"

"After a week of constant demands, I do not look forward to adding more work."

He narrowed his eyes as he looked at me, "That sounds almost truthful."

"Why would that surprise you?" The corner of my lip tucked up, "I'm a minster's daughter; I'm always truthful."

"No, sorry, I've known too many PKs. Usually pastor's kids have learned to prevaricate."

"Stereotyping tends to say more about the speaker than the subject."

He thought about that, "Nope. Fact."

"Based on your experience, which—unless you've known a vast number of children with minsters for a parent over your, what, thirty-three years or whatever—then yours is a rather limited experience."

"How do you know I didn't conduct a survey?"

I laughed.

"Yeah, because surveys are notoriously accurate."

"You have a nice laugh."

Startled, I stared at him, "Uh, thanks?"

"You're welcome." Jefferson replied, "About the job…."

"I'm sorry, I can't do it. Beth is really good, and her fee is reasonable. Be leery of those who charge too much or too little. The quality doesn't always match the price; some offer a low price and provide low quality, and some charge too much and offer, well, low quality."

I stood up, my body had grown numb with the cold. My leg, that pesky thorn in the flesh, collapsed under my weight. Jefferson grabbed my arm, lending support despite remaining seated.

"You alright?"

"I'm fine. Thank you."

I pulled away with a grateful, if embarrassed, smile.

He stood up, returning the chair to the table.

"Shall we go inside? I have some ideas for the website."

"Not going to work." I walked around him to the door, "Nice try."

I felt him at my back as I opened the door.

"Really, lay off the pushiness."

"I wanted to make sure you got inside okay," he protested.

I threw him a dirty look over my shoulder. He was right there, in my space. "I'm good. Thanks."

"I know you are good, that's why I want you to make me a website."

"Good graces," I mumbled under my breath.

"Take as long as you want," he added. "I've only started playing around with the idea of selling online."

I hadn't entered the house in order to block him from doing so. I closed the door again. I stepped back, figuring he would also, but instead hit his front. Ouch. Hard chest.

"Personal space. In America that means a good a three feet around a person," I commented when he didn't move.

"Hey, you knew I was here when you back up," his breath hit my ear as he lowered his voice. "I don't mind, really."

Each step I take appears to place me in his path, literally in this case. Rather stupid move on my part, stepping back.

Surprised at my lack of panic that a strange man would push himself inside my house, I berated myself for carelessness. After all, I knew of nothing of him.

I opened the door, my mouth in a thin line. He followed me inside, stopping in the back room and shutting the door after him.

Surprised at my lack of panic that a strange man would push himself inside my house, I berated myself for carelessness. After all, I knew of nothing of him.

Head bowed, I walked through the dining room into the living room. Selecting the overstuffed chair positioned near the front window, I sat down, making sure I had my phone in my hand. From my position, I had a clear line of sight to the back room.

The square wooden coffee table matched the dining room table, both having stone inlaid on top. I had arranged the room with the coffee table positioned in front of the sofa, which was against the wall, with the chair being close enough that I could reach it. The low table held several books I'd been reading.

Jefferson came over and sat on the couch that lined the wall.

"At this point, it's no longer being pushy," I didn't look at him.

"If it matters so much, I'll design your website. If you can tell me, no evasiveness, why you are so determined that I do it. Less than two weeks ago, we were strangers passing in the woods."

"I work better with someone who is nearby, not communicating through e-mails. It's really that simple."

Tension melted from my neck, but I kept ahold of my phone.

"Fine. Enough. Let me get my laptop; we can work in the kitchen."

I saw a flash of triumph on his face, which made perverse me want to backtrack and toss him out. Based on how well he'd listened to me thus far, I felt leery of giving him what he wanted.

That wariness could not defeat my need to test myself. Maybe some part of me felt that, if I interact with him, he may turn human in my mind and no longer exist as a player in tragic play. I had already observed his attempts at being charming, his light flirting, and his determination. One could say he had attempted to manipulate me with his charm.

Retrieving my laptop, I set it up on the dining room table. I offered him a drink before starting. I sat down, angling the computer so he could see it as well. I spent the next few hours going over different website designs, asking what exactly he expected and stating what I could deliver and the fee. At least it felt like hours. I closed the laptop and gave him an estimate of when I would have something to show him.

"That's sooner than I expected." Jefferson rose.

"I'm making this a priority," I stood, as well, heading toward the back door, "I'll text you if I need more time or am ready earlier. Any questions you have, feel free to text me."

I held the back door open.

"Thank you," he said, almost meekly. Feeling ashamed for his pushiness?

"You're welcome."

I shut the door after him.

CHAPTER 7

A Small-Town Church

Is this the issue? An inability to forgive the man whose mistake cost us our parents?

Funny, this is one of the questions I asked myself. Not why can't I forgive the man, but why did I- forgive (yeah, yeah, oops), the continuing mystery. But no, this isn't the forgiveness issue I struggle with. Grief, yes. Every day.

I've read many grief books, attended meetings, and yet nothing worked as well as time. It took time for the numbness to fade. Losing a parent, even both parents, is common enough that you encounter lots of empathy. At my age, still in college, there were discreet and not so discreet questions about whether I would still attend the expensive private college, switch to a community college, or quit college and get a job.

True to my contrary nature, I dodged these questions. Those who knew my parents also knew that they came from money. Mom and Dad were only children and orphans, for even adults can claim that label. I do. Sorry, anyhow, Mom inherited from her grandparents, sharing with relatives who are only shadows in my memory. Dad was the last of his line, until Jeremy and I, and so he had no one to share with. He invested his money, as well as Mom's, and starting a family later in life allowed them to gather more of a nest egg. Once aspiring to a career in law, Dad kept enough of an interest in that to ensure that, if something ever happened to him or Mom, or both, his children would be provided for.

My college tuition was provided for through a trust. Jeremy handled the financial arrangements until my twenty-second birthday, but I have to be honest and admit that I never got a handle on the financial angles, not like he had. Sometimes Jeremy forced me to listen as he explained what was happening to my money. I still didn't get it. Okay, well, in the end, I understand enough to manage it as I grew older. I even managed to increase the amount saved since I worked, paying for my needs that way.

Mom once told me that while saving money was ideal, do not skimp on quality. Those $20 shoes may appear to be a steal, but you will replace those several times before the $100 ones wear out. If you chose correctly, of course. My clothes were always well made, but not pricey, our furniture simple, but lasting. I followed that example well into my adult years.

How is this for side tracking?

So now, nothing left but grief. Every time I found, find, myself remembering Mom's lessons or the way Dad did something, the sparks of painful guilt still surface.

As I wrote, my parents died in a car accident. They were hit in an intersection by a truck running the red light. The driver thought it was a yellow light and, when he hit the car, Dad died on impact. The car spun out into the oncoming traffic from the other direction. There were injuries to other drivers and passengers, but my parents were the only deaths. Mom died as the EMTs arrived.

The man was brought up on vehicular manslaughter charges. I protested when Jeremy wanted to put in a plea of mercy, spewing bitter words at him for even considering asking for a lighter sentence. He took my words—undeserved accusations—without anger, as symbols of grief, accepting my sobbing apologies later. My brother had a way about him of not making you ashamed of your hatred as much as gently guiding you to mercy. The driver ended up taking a plea bargain, lessening his sentence.

With Jeremy as my example, I forgave that man for killing my parents. It took time. The Internet allowed me to check on that driver; he's out of prison, and his Facebook profile shows him with children. I never believed he understood the pain Jeremy and I felt, and I pray his children won't either for a long time. I guess there's mercy in me.

So, yes, reading over this before posting it, I think I discovered one clue. I had Jeremy then, and I followed his example in forgiveness. A simple excuse; I needed a role model.

Isn't that role model supposed to be Jesus? Or does the familiarity with what He forgave—the betrayals and insults, the misunderstandings and refusals to change—lessen the power of meaning in our own lives?

I would believe the latter if fewer eyes had been damp during Christ's resurrection service. and if my own eyes had stopped leaking when I looked at His cross.

No, perhaps for me it comes down to intent. The man who ran the light made a choice, conscious or unconscious, that resulted in consequences for more than himself. But he did not wake up making that decision. In a heartbeat, the moment of choice was over with instantaneous, disastrous results.

How do you forgive someone who keeps walking down the road of bad choices, each step a tear in the heart of one you love?
—ReesesCup76, The Cost of Forgiving Blog

Living near a small town, I nevertheless felt immune to the way I heard that people in small towns acted. I may have heard whispers of gossip when I occasionally attended the tiny church in town but, keeping to myself, I assumed I kept me above the whispers.

It's rather disconcerting when you discover that people have been discussing you. As a child, I knew everyone watched how the pastor's kid behaved. Years removed from that environment, accustomed to a life where people left you alone if you left them alone, I'd forgotten that I could stir someone's interest.

No longer as a pastor's kid, but as a stranger. The small church was worlds removed from the politics of the church and the up-and-coming workers for God. I felt safe from anyone knowing my dad. Even the small-town mentality of our growing denomination hadn't touched this area.

Huh, small-town mentality. Would hiding in a city have been better? I depended on being excluded from the social hub of the area, with my lack of family ties. When encountered, many townspeople did, in fact, act courteously, but faintly aloof. Not enough. Sprinkled among the tight-knit community were a few affable souls. Ellen had claimed my friendship early on—amazing still how easily that happened, and I could not resist the saints of the church. Found among those women and men were ones who burdened themselves with acting as the arms and legs of the church; every event or funding drive had their names listed there: those who quietly beat as the heart.

Those hearts were the ones whose greetings rang with sincerity, who may have teased but did not cut with their jokes. When the church members grumbled in the background about Mom homeschooling me, one woman mentioned to Mom how Mary taught Jesus at home. With a squeeze of Mom's arm, she walked away with a smile. Simple support, without engaging in debate. So small a comment, yet Mom related to Dad how much it had meant.

At one church, every Sabbath, I engaged in teasing with an elderly man. I greeted him with a hug and asked him how he was. Every Sabbath, he would sigh and reply, "Terrible, just terrible." When pressed, he would relate various ailments with a twinkle in his eye.

I matured fast and, at eleven, looked a few years older. Someone decided my hugging him wasn't appropriate, no idea why. They mentioned it to Mom, who gently suggested I stop, given my age. That hurt, that taste of judgment. The next Sabbath, for the first time, I didn't greet "Terrible Charlie" with a hug. My face must have reflected my emotions, and he asked what was wrong. With the honesty of a child, I told him. With a stern expression, he looked around us, then he hugged me.

I never heard another comment.

Why are people so eager to destroy innocence? With relief I discovered most churches lack the—well, no word for it—of that particular church. Still, there are so many other areas where that sin exists in the mind of the watcher.

When I attended the church in this small town, I found myself drawn to these hearts again. They were the reason I found myself up front reading the Bible texts or teaching in the Sabbath school rooms. Still, I managed to keep a certain distance, until the church's Christmas play. At the reception afterwards, Mrs. Childers, a fifty-something woman with dyed brown hair, trim figure, and soft voice, mentioned she heard I was working for Jefferson Fisher. We sat next to each other at one of the round tables set up in the basement of the church.

"That's good that you two are getting to know each other." Mrs. Childers reached out and patted my arm, her doll-face lit with a smile, "He's been alone too long."

"You know him?" Perplexed, I added, "I've never heard anyone mention him before."

"Oh, yes. His grandparents used to attend our church, Jeff and his siblings along with them when they visited."

"I see," I politely smiled. First time I had heard about siblings. Doesn't matter.

"He stopped coming three years or so ago." Not deterred by my disinterest, Mrs. Childers added, "Maybe you two will find things in common."

The need to be left alone, perhaps? Not that he's been displaying that desire, as he was texting me regularly with ideas or questions during time I told him the project would take. Good thing I finished. I planned on informing him tomorrow.

Several other women at the table joined in, giving me a sale pitch, as if Jefferson was a car I had thought about buying. A few held an opinion that I needed someone in my life, to make me open up. Not that they said exactly that. No, that would have been pushy.

"Jefferson's like his granddad; he values his privacy."

Across the table, a sinewy middle-aged man with rigid posture met my eyes. I noted his broad face, browned even in winter, and stiff, grizzled hair. How much gel did he used? Bristly hair covered his lower face, almost concealing the annoyed look on his lips.

"Oh, Reisa isn't a gossip." Mrs. Childers rushed to say, "You know better than that, Obe."

Obadiah Richards, Ellen had mentioned him, pointing out his truck on the dirt road as he came to visit Jefferson. I'd seen it since then, given Jefferson's and my shared driveway. Apparently they were friends. Jefferson isn't the loner Ellen had made him out to be.

"I value my privacy as well, Mr. Richards." I stood up, grabbing my bag from the floor, "If you will excuse me, I should head home."

Exchanging good-byes with a couple of people, I headed up the stairs, grabbing my coat from the wall near the front door.

"I hope I haven't offended you," Obadiah said, standing off to the side, watching me struggle with my coat. "Here, let me help."

"Thanks," I handed him my bag and put on the coat. Taking the bag back, I told him, "No worries. I'm not offended. You have a good night."

I moved to the front doors, but Obadiah rushed to open one for me.

"Thank you." I walked to my truck, Obadiah following behind. Um, why?

"Is there something you need?" I asked him.

"I didn't realize who you were," he looked sheepish, "Thought you were another one of those single gals the church ladies are always trying to push on Jeff."

"Well, I am single." I flashed a grin, "That's an offensive state to some, I'm gathering. Don't they know we've moved beyond 'be fruitful and multiply?' Besides, I take after Paul rather than Solomon." I opened the door and tossed my bag in.

"Jeff said you were mindin' your own business."

"Easier than mindin' someone else's."

Climbing into the truck, I met Obadiah's puzzled gaze, "I believe I taught your son Eric in the Teens class. Nice and polite. You raised him well."

"Thank you, We're proud of him."

"Good night, Mr. Richards."

He ran a hand over his beard, still eying me.

"Call me Obe, Ms. Jensen."

"Then call me Reisa. See you next Sabbath."

I shut the door and started the truck. Obe stepped back as I pulled out of the parking space. Waving at him, I drove off.

CHAPTER 8

Bible Words

Dad loved languages, especially the original languages of the Bible. One could find books on classical Hebrew, Aramaic, and Greek languages in our house, as well as flashcards and workbooks. Dad took it upon himself to instruct his daughter as well as offering a class for interested church members. He felt you could understand the Bible better if you read it as it was originally written.

Lacking my father's ear and eye for languages, I still managed to remember some of those words. For example, the words "forgive" and "forgiveness" are the translations of three Hebrew words, "kaphar," "nake," and "saletch."

Originally, "kaphar" meant "to cover," "to cover over," or "to overspread." Genesis 6:14 uses the word in that context. As a noun, "kaphar" signifies a place of shelter, sometimes signifying a village, e.g., Caper-naum (village of Nahum).

Over fifty percent of the time in the Bible, it's translated as "to atone" or "to make atonement." The cover of the Ark, the mercy seat, is the noun "kapporeth," derived from "kaphar."

"Kaphar" has been also translated "purge," when "purge away" is given as the translation, suggesting that making atonement is strongly connected with purging sins.

Three times "kaphar" is used to express the idea "forgive:" in Deuteronomy, pleading for God to forgive Israel, absolving them of the guilt of innocent blood; in Psalms, when God forgave or covered, Israel's iniquity in Egypt and the desert; And lastly, when Jeremiah spoke against those who were against him as God's prophet, asking God not to cover their sins. No atonement for them.

Forgiveness is connected to the idea of covering with blood. The blood of Jesus covers our sins, allowing forgiveness.

I love the word "naga," which first means "lifting," second, "carrying," and third, "taking away of a burden."

And doesn't sinning leave you feeling weighed down? Being hurt, well, it's like carrying boulders. The idea of something lifting that weight and taking away that boulder entices.

"Naga" also represents acceptance, as it is used thirteen times in the Old Testament. Fifteen passages have "naga" translated as "forgive," each time implying that the sin is taken away. When the Jewish priest made atonement for the congregation by eating the sin offering, he "bore" the iniquity of the people. As Christ did.

That leaves us with the word "saletch." It appears roughly fifty times, translated thirty-three times as "forgive," twice as "forgiveness," once as "spare," and fourteen times as "pardon." Each time it is used, it expresses the divine pardon extended to the sinner, God to man, not man to man.

> God not only pardons us from sin, but reclaims us. Time and again, the Bible records God's forgiveness toward humankind. He reclaims us and remakes us, forgiving us and connecting us to Him again.

God not only pardons us from sin, but reclaims us. Time and again, the Bible records God's forgiveness toward humankind. He reclaims us and remakes us, forgiving us and connecting us to Him again.

Sin not only separates us from God, it also separates us from each other. One would think that a group with a common disease—sin in this case—would unite under the common ailment.

> *Sin doesn't unite; it rips apart. It tears flesh from hearts, destroying compassion with the rage for revenge. Cain killed Abel, and we have been killing each other with words and actions ever since.*
>
> *Our sins against God are so huge—heavy enough to kill the Son of God with the burden—so with them being forgiven, forgiving the smaller sins against each other should be easy, shouldn't it?*
>
> *Wrong.*
>
> —ReesesCup76, The Cost of Forgiving Blog

Body twisted in blankets, I struggled a bit to free myself. Cold air kissed my bare legs once I exposed them, raising goosebumps. Sitting up, I swung my legs to the side of the bed, flexing my neck and shoulders. Carefully getting to my feet, I winced nonetheless. Physical therapy, various medicines, and two years hadn't made much difference. To my leg or to my heart.

I snatched the cane next to the bed, the one a friend had custom ordered for me, with a carved raven as a handle. With the cold weather, my leg seemed worse. Perhaps hiking wasn't the best activity. Not that I'd been on the trail much the last week or so.

Using the cane as an aid, I got to my feet. Taking my robe off the hook on the closet door, I wrapped myself in its fluffy warmth. I went down the hallway to my office and opened up my laptop. As I waited for it to wake up, I looked through the window.

The moon lit up the winter night, making the thin layer of snow that had snuck down over the last day glisten. This window faced the back yard, allowing me to view the forest. Sometimes I saw deer wandering to where the garden once thrived.

The laptop finished booting, and I opened up my e-mail. Plenty of e-mails, some even not ads, but not one from Jefferson. A week ago, I texted him that I had finished the site, with no response. I waited two days, then tried to call. Finally, I used the e-mail address he had given me. Seemed like he wasn't answering that either. Strange how he went from texting me all the time to zero contact. Well, short of walking over to his house, I'd tried.

Right. I rubbed my forehead, so life would stop taunting me. Plus, I had taken time from other projects to work on this. I should go over there to make sure I can file the job away as "done." A glance at the time confirmed that it was officially Christmas, in fact, almost morning. Perhaps he was busy with family. I knew his grandparents were gone, but no one said his parents were, and those at church had mentioned his siblings.

I answered the few personal e-mails, catching up with some friends, and left the business-related ones for later. Going to my main blog, I put up a Merry Christmas message, then went to my other blog and poured out some of the thoughts that were keeping me awake.

When my brain turned to mush, my eyes blurring on the screen, I closed everything down and shut off the laptop. At some point I should buy another desktop, keeping this laptop for my story writing. And games.

The sky was changing, heralding the sun with traces of pink in the lightening sky. Beautiful.

Stretching in the chair, I grabbed the cane I had left leaning against the desk and stood up. Briefly I debated going to church; it was sure to have a larger crowd today. Visiting children and grandchildren—as well as those who skipped church the rest of the year—habitually attended the Christmas service. With Christmas falling on Sabbath this year, perhaps the amount of people would decrease from earlier years.

That thought, along with guilt about wanting to skip church on Christ's birthday—not that it was the real day, of course,—made me get into the shower. I took my time getting ready, selecting a red lace dress that fell to midcalf. With its long sleeves and high neckline, I thought it modest enough for church when I had brought it online. It had a tunic red cloth lining, except for the sleeves and around the neck.

Examining myself in the full-length mirror hanging on my bedroom door, I bit my lip uncertainly. It looked festive, with traces of sexiness. The latter gave me pause. I had let my hair down and had only a touch of makeup around my eyes. Somehow, I knew my mother would disapprove of the dress. Funny how I cared now—years after she had died—how she felt about my clothes, when I had spent my teenage years resisting her.

I slipped on some kitten heels, red like my dress, and sprayed on some light perfume. Mom taught me to present my best before God in His house. That was what I was doing.

A quick breakfast and I arrived at church in time to snag the last parking spot. Others started pulling onto the grass as I got out. Putting my Bible in my overlarge bag, I shouldered the bag and took my cane with me as I got out. Vanity had no place at church, and I found myself needing that aid.

Ellen smiled at me through the glass doors of the church as I hobbled up. The greeter held the door open with his own smile, wrinkling up his face.

Thanking him and taking a bulletin from another man, I smiled at Ellen as we walked toward the sanctuary.

"I thought you were visiting family."

"We all decided to come here for Christmas. I planned to invite you over this afternoon." She beamed at me.

"Planned?"

"Well, you may have another invitation coming. Don't ask; I'm not telling from whom."

She slipped away.

I huffed a breath. what was she up to?

Since I wasn't teaching a class this morning, I seated myself in the adult class that was meeting near the front of the sanctuary. This one was more traditional, closely following the adult quarterly. How the church had enough people to warrant two adult classes, I do not know, but they did.

Ellen plopped herself next to me, smoothing down her purple crushed-velvet dress. I smiled at her.

"Nice dress."

"Thank you." She beamed once again, "Yours is quite becoming. I've never seen you in a dress before."

"Thanks, I prefer wearing dress pants to church, but this dress appeared appropriate for Christmas."

"I should go help my daughter, she's in the cradle roll class with her three, but I wanted to chat a moment with you. It has been a while."

Retrieving my Bible from my bag, I leaned my cane against the pew in front of me, "How's the family?"

"Oh, good, I planned to introduce you all after church. Did Jefferson get ahold of you?"

My mouth thinned, "Yes, to my surprise. I do not remember telling you I designed websites."

"Oh, you did. When I told you my youngest was having trouble with the website he built, you gave some recommendations, if you recall."

Vaguely I did and reprimanded myself suitably.

"I hope I didn't overstep, giving Jeff your name."

Her long face sharpened, watching my reaction.

"Nope, not at all. Thanks for tossing work my way."

I opened the bulletin.

"You are annoyed," her voice trembled slightly, "I'm sorry. I thought perhaps…." Her voice drifted off, and she cleared her throat.

Oh, well , it's Christmas. I reached out and squeezed the hand laying primly on her leg. "No, it's all good."

She perked up at my warm tone, "You two are both alone; you may find something in common."

I withdrew my hand. "Others have had the same thought. I didn't know his grandparents were members of the church."

"Oh, yes, and their parents before them. We have a nice little cluster of Adventists here."

The corner of my lip lifted, "Imagine that."

Mr. Davis stood in front of the pews, "Good morning, happy Sabbath, and Merry Christmas to you all."

Ellen jumped up. "Oh, I need to help Mabel," she whispered. "Excuse me."

She demurely rushed down the aisle of the church, an interesting combination that few have mastered.

Fighting a smile, I opened up my quarterly.

CHAPTER 9

The Fisher Family

Shame covers the offender, whether he's aware of it or not. When one betrays, no mark lies visibly upon your forehead. When you break God's law, unless others witness the act, none can tell upon seeing you. I witnessed the act of transgression; I saw the cost of the sin. If we had seen the repercussions of our selfishness, would that have stopped us?

If we knew that some carry a burden because we have hurt them to the point that they doubt they can forgive, would that prevent the transgression? We weigh each other down with sins' fruits. Placing anchors around each other's hearts.

Who is more to blame, those who sin or those who refuse to release the burden by forgiving? Standing before God, can I justify my stone heart by pointing to those who destroyed the ones I loved?
—ReesesCup76, The Cost of Forgiving Blog

The pastor was serving one of the larger sister churches today, leaving the head elder to hold the Christmas service. No potluck followed the service, as food was waiting at home for many in the congregation, and so after church the parking lot was flooded with people rushing home. I limped over to my truck to wait for Mr. Davis. A few Sabbaths back, he had offered me half a cord of wood after I had mentioned waiting to use my little stove because I haven't purchased any wood. Forget about me chopping my own. He had dutifully brought the wood the next Sabbath, but I wasn't there. Cut to today. Waving aside my apologies, he had offered to load up my truck after church.

What the Pharisees would have had to say about this Sabbath labor I do not know, but no one here batted an eye as Mr. Davis pulled up next to me and loaded up the truck bed. A few even rolled up their sleeves to help him. Several offered to come over the next day to help me stack the wood, but I declined with a smile.

"Thank you," I said, as Mr. Davis shut the tailgate.

"No problem, girlie," His eyes crinkled, "You have a good Christmas, yah hear?" His southwestern accent showing through. He was a transplant, like myself, having met his wife at college and then following her back to her hometown.

"You, too."

Mr. Davis climbed into his truck as I returned a wave from his wife.

Oh, no. She's waving me over. Cheeks flushed, I walked that way.

Powering down the window, she stuck out her head, "You got plans for lunch? Sue's back at the house making ours; we would love to have you."

"You wouldn't be intruding, but I won't press you." Her attention had been caught by some standing nearby., and she quickly added, "Good to see y'all. We should get out of the way. Merry Christmas!"

The Davises drove off as I turned to see whom she was referring to.

A family of "gazelles," all lanky legged and slim. Even their heads matched with reddish tints to their light-brown hair. They stood by the tailgate of my truck, watching me with curious eyes.

I searched my memory, had we been introduced? Hmm.

The answer arrived when Jefferson joined the group. Lacking his normal headgear for on the trail, I noticed that his hair color matched the others, as did his physique. Brilliantly, I deduced that this was his family. A car honked as it passed and the older man in the group walked over and bent down to talk through the open window to whomever was inside.

One down, four to go.

"Hello," I offered.

Jefferson smiled at me, "Merry Christmas."

"Merry Christmas," I automatically replied, "I didn't see you in church."

"We were running behind, slipped in the back," A woman in a heavy wool coat, hair laced with gray, replied. "Excuse our rudeness, I'm Ginger Fisher, Jefferson's mother. These are my daughters, Lindsey and Kathryn, and my younger son Nathan."

I leaned against the truck and held out my hand, shaking each hand firmly. "Nice to meet you, Reisa Jensen."

"Oh, we know. Jeff told us about you. You bought the Millers' house."

A frown creased Mrs. Fisher's brow, "It's rather sad about Mr. Miller's passing."

"That's correct and yes," I offered a tentative smile.

"You run the Introvert Review," Nathan, looking like a younger version of Jefferson, piped up.

Smile gone, "Er, I do not recall telling…."

"We looked you up." Lindsey interrupted.

I eyed the slim girl, her angular face turning slightly mischievous. I googled myself upon occasion, checking my footprint. My main site does appear, as well as guest posts I've done on other blogs. Nothing about the accident, thankfully, popped up on the first page. Most people, unless really curious, rarely checked more than the first two pages of a search, if even that. If they did, well, not much is hidden on the Internet if you know where to look?

Mrs. Fisher's face flushed, "I'm sorry. With you buying the Millers house, I mean, single women do not usually settle in this area," she mumbled.

The older man rejoined us, holding out his hand, "Bert Fisher."

I shook his hand, warily offering a greeting.

"Well, you are a looker, aren't you?" he grinned.

Oh, dear Father, help me out of this.

I lifted my chin, feeling my cheeks warming, "Thank you for the compliment. I'm sorry, I should go…."

"Oh, no, do you have plans? We were hoping we could talk you into coming over for dinner. Ellen said you would be free," Mrs. Fisher divulged.

Ellen. Dang it, woman.

"Ellen's a sweetheart, but mistaken. Nice meeting you all."

Jefferson broke his silence, "Please? I want to go over a few things about the website with you."

"Another day," I replied, "It's Christmas."

Mrs. Fisher whispered something to Mr. Fisher, and he strolled off. Really, did they marry because of their similar looks? Mr. Fisher's head was covered in gray, otherwise he fit the required appearance.

"This is awkward," Mrs. Fisher said to me, "We are normally not so rude, and forgive us if we are being too forward, but Ellen said you had no family."

A pang shot through my heart, and my vision darkened. "Ellen said that?" I scanned the parking lot and grass area, mostly empty of cars. Ellen stood off to the side, observing us. I met her eyes across the parking lot, berating myself for befriending a gossip. Didn't I realize it would bite me? Hadn't I seen that happen to Mom?

Ellen looked away, her red face visible even from space.

Fixing a neutral smile on my lips, I searched for a way to remain polite. Wasn't that my problem? The manners drilled into my head stood in the way of solitude. Not to mention my leg protesting my standing position.

> *I searched for a way to remain polite. Wasn't that my problem? The manners drilled into my head stood in the way of solitude.*

"I'm sorry," Jefferson broke the awkward pause, "we are being pushy. Mom, let's go. If you change your mind, Reisa, you know where the house is."

Mr. Fisher pulled up, and Jefferson firmly escorted his mother into the passenger seat. The girls, with apologetic looks toward me, climbed into the sedan's back seat. They drove off with mumbled good-byes while Nathan remained next to my truck.

"Go ahead and get into my car," Jefferson said, tossing his keys to Nathan, who skillfully caught them.

"I like your website, and I understand the whole introvert part." Nathan winked at me before walking off, leaving Jefferson and I alone.

Jefferson moved so that he could lean against the truck, as he rubbed the back of his neck. A car drove by; Ellen was in the passenger seat, her face averted.

"Don't hold it against her," Jefferson said. "She's fond of you and worries about you being alone."

I tensed, poking my tongue lightly into my cheek and inhaling a long breath, as I stared at Jefferson. Five years, Ellen said, he had lived here, in isolation. I had lived here ten months, with no one bothering me, and now it had ended. The church, I understand them growing friendlier the longer I'm here, but how did Jefferson pull off five years of solitude?

"Five years. I would have settled for a full year," I mumbled.

"Sorry?" He tilted his head in question.

I waved a hand in dismissal.

"Never mind that," I paused, trying to rearrange my thoughts. "Ellen worried about you as well, and I stayed out of it. As much as I appreciate—well, not quite that—as nice as it seems, I'm good. Please stop."

His posture changed as I talked. He stopped leaning on my truck and stiffened his body along with his face.

"I apologize," he said in a curt tone.

Matching his curtness, I informed him, "Your website is done. The information you need is in my e-mail to you."

I know friendliness, it is kind, like Mr. Davis. What this was, well, it looked akin to interest. My stomach soured.

"I told you to leave her alone," Nathan said to Jefferson. He had driven Jefferson's SUV over, windows down. "Sorry, he can be a bit stubborn when he wants something."

Nathan gave me a sheepish look. as he added, "You are rather pretty, you know. That's a great dress." A great dress that I'm now donating.

With a cynical laugh I replied, "That makes sense, Vivian was rather weak."

I bit my lip, holding back the rest of the leak. No wonder people know more than I thought because I had inadvertently peaked their interest.

As I suspected, Jefferson's manners were as ingrained as mine, and he rushed to open the truck door for me.

"Thank you." I slid in, leaning the cane against my bag in the passenger seat.

"Merry Christmas." I peeked my head out to yell to Nathan. I repeated the wish to Jefferson before pulling the door from his hands.

He knocked on the window. Reluctantly, I rolled it down.

"You are sending mixed signals, you know." He leaned on the door, "Are you mad or what?"

"Being nice isn't the same as offering an invitation," I replied. Starting the truck up, I added, "You might want to have your brother move."

"We aren't done."

I took the truck out of park into reverse, pressing the gas, slowly rolling back. Jefferson walked along with me until I was inches from his SUV.

"I have great insurance. Do you?" I said with a smirk.

He looked uneasy.

"Kidding. Please move."

He crossed his arms, "Just a moment more."

Jefferson's smugness vanished under my challenging stare, my foot lifting off the brake.

"Please, wait a second, alright?"

"Don't," I called after him as he turned to motion to Nathan. He ignored my comment. As soon as Nathan moved forward, I backed up then pulled alongside the SUV. Nathan grinned at me as I waved to him before leaving the parking lot.

CHAPTER 10

Nicole

When we buried our parents, Jeremy and I discovered the extent of our parents' influence. Person after person, until they blurred together in my mind, told us how Dad or Mom witnessed to them, helped them, or befriended them. Roy Boltz' 'thank you' sounded through my thoughts, foretelling, perhaps, my parents' experience when Christ brings them home.

They weren't perfect, my parents, but grace carried them through. What would Dad have said to his daughter who nursed bitterness in her heart? I cannot claim I influenced anyone. I can barely claim politeness when inwardly I want to flee. I can discuss the Bible; a childhood of hearing religious discussions plus years of studying on my own make my grounding sound, if not perfectly level.

Sometimes I play "The Motions"[2] by Matthew West, singing along, tears in my eyes. The motions are what I have left.

I have no doubt I'm trapped in this cage of memories, missing so many...especially missing him. If Elijah haven't died, would

---

[2] West, Matthew; Mizell, Sam; Houser, Jason. "The Motions." ©Word Music, LLC.

I have ever noticed this cherished resentment? He made me so happy, I loved him so much; he overshadowed my self-awareness.

I miss Elijah most of all. It feels disloyal to acknowledge that, but missing El makes the rest of the losses ache more. Did God use Elijah's death as a well to bring my sin to the light? Is not forgiving a sin?

—ReesesCup76, The Cost of Forgiving Blog

New Year's came and went; I heard nothing from Ellen. Jefferson sent me payment for the website, thanking me in a formal e-mail for the work I had done. Rebuffing someone's kindness felt wrong, but the question remained if it was kindness. Plus, how else could I get him to leave me alone?

Selene, when I called to wish her a Merry Christmas, informed me that, in a romance novel she was reading, Jefferson was the ideal hero. That Selene, the nonfiction aficionado, reading a romance novel surprised me. The fact that said romance novels presented pushiness as a romantic option disappointed me. Growing up, I had devoured any books within reach, including romance novels, but I never read ones with the heroes Selene talked about—ones who forced their own family on a neighbor they did not know, because of simple attraction.

Yeah, I did not know that last part for sure. Fears given voice perhaps.

The first Sabbath of the New Year found me in Michigan, visiting Lee and her family. I needed to see a happy life, her happy life in particular. God sent Andrew into her life, a pastor with a temper, who offered empathy without expectations. I believe their friendship turning into love shocked them more than anyone else. After all the pain she had suffered and the understandable confusion and borderline destructive coping mechanisms that came with it, she had finally found peace.

Seeing her with her baby and adoring husband, someone else would assume her life had been easy. There were still shadows in those eyes, but that precious little girl was slowly healing her mother's heart.

Andy showed an interest in my current study on forgiveness, debating and disputing certain aspects of my opinions.

"That's why they are called *opinions*," I smirked, "because you aren't required to share them."

Andy rolled his eyes, choosing to walk away, Lee giggling at his expression. Oh, he's fun to rile up.

Mid-January found me working on another ad campaign, followed by editing for publication a collection of short stories previously published on my blog. I caught up on my book reviews, since I had always managed to find time to read; I just needed to blog my opinions.

Ellen never contacted me after our visual exchange in the parking lot on Christmas day. I felt her to be a coward. Aren't gossips cowards at heart? Talking behind someone's back doesn't require courage. At church, Ellen slipped away, squinty-eyed, whenever I came close to her. The other members were still friendly, so it was all good. No one mentioned Jefferson to me, although I caught Mrs. Childers telling Mrs. Kelley, "Just call me Sue Ann, sweetie; Reisa's pretty, but Ellen says she's too much of a loner for Jeff. Too bad, Jeff's finally ready to settle down, and there aren't too many girls around here for him."

Her face turned beet red when she saw me.

Under the laugh I fought to keep inside, I felt strange. I didn't want Jefferson settling down. He had broken something; let him stay restless. In the end, I pretended I didn't hear, despite all three of us, me, Mrs. Childers, and Mrs. Kelley, knowing full well I had.

February came around, bringing an unseasonably warm day that led me to the forest, carrying along my Canon. The early morning sun lit up the melting forest. The blue, white, and browns with hints of green from the pine trees encouraged me to fill my SD card.

As I lowered my camera, I heard footfalls behind me. Nathan came up the hill, a smile growing on his face as he saw me. Farther along, behind Nathan, Jeff's face had a contrasting expression, scowling. Another figure came up behind them, dark hair spilling from underneath a wool hat, excluding her as one of their sisters.

I moved off the path to let them by, suspecting all the while that Nathan wouldn't take the hint. Sure enough, he stopped.

"You never mentioned being a photographer on your site," Nathan said.

"It's a hobby," I replied. "My websites are about books anyway."

"May I see your camera?"

"Sure," I passed over my camera just as Jefferson and the woman reached us.

"Reisa," Jefferson nodded, his face blank.

I smiled at him, feeling impish.

"Jefferson."

Reaching out my hand, covered in a fingerless glove, I introduced myself to the woman once it was apparent that Jefferson wouldn't.

"Reisa Jensen."

"Um, I'm Nicole." She cast an uncertain look at Jefferson before shaking my hand. She was pretty, with soft brown eyes, espresso-colored hair and mocha skin.

"Nice to meet you. Please stop," I added to Nathan as he flipped through my photos.

"You're pretty good," Nathan told me, unperturbed by my frown. He held up the camera, a photo filling the LCD screen.

Jefferson stepped around me, taking the camera. "You didn't mention you knew about photography."

"Jeff's a professional photographer," Nicole informed me.

I nodded, "I'm aware. I'm an aspiring amateur."

"You want to be a professional?" Nicole asked.

"No, I'm aspiring to be an amateur," I grinned, "Too many people nowadays want to be a professional. I say aim lower, easier to reach your goal. Can I have my camera, please?"

"Yeah, sure," Jefferson handed it over, his expression contemplative.

"So you taught yourself?" Nathan inquired.

"No, my brother taught me." My smile deflated. "He loved photography. He used to spend hours snapping photos, then more hours in the darkroom."

"He didn't like digital?" Nicole asked, then didn't pause for my answer, continuing, "I know some people prefer film, but I personally think you can't beat the convenience of instant results. Jeff uses both."

"You said your brother used to," Nathan spoke. "No longer?"

I swallowed a lump.

"He died before the good quality digital SLRs became affordable. I still think he would have preferred film. The patience involved appealed to him."

"I'm sorry," Nathan responded, his brow furrowed.

"Yeah, sorry," Jefferson added, looking concerned. Nicole moved to Jefferson's side, offering me a small smile of sympathy as she threaded her hand with Jefferson's.

"Thanks. Well," I drew a deep breath, steadying myself, "have a good hike."

"Later," Nathan replied, saluting me. I shook my head at him. Jefferson watched me, Nicole hanging on to his arm, as I turned to walk away.

CHAPTER 11

The Grocery Store

When I was young, before my brother went to academy, though sometimes even after he did, I would curl up in his bed. We would talk about anything and everything. Whatever subject interested him, he try out his new knowledge on me. I learned about electricity, the planets, and various battles in history years before I encountered those subjects in school.

Jeremy listened as much as he talked. I chattered about bugs, how I learned to jump rope, and other things of interest to a young child. When I was older, I talked about the books I had read. We discussed our various interpretations of the classics, debating the successes and failures of various authors.

More often, as I grew, Jeremy became a sounding board for my internal struggles. I wondered aloud why I lack the sweetness of Mom. Why there was a sarcastic edge to my humor. You know, Jeremy would comfort me, never lying or offering glib words. I could have squeezed myself into someone else's image, losing parts of myself, or I could accept the flawed but kind person he saw in me.

"We are all flawed," he often said. "Even a sweet tone can conceal unkind words."

I observe people, enjoy guessing their personalities from a snapshot of time. Sometimes I end up knowing these people and *am able to check my observations; but other times, these people are forever defined in my mind by what they may have been on a good day or bad day. Nonetheless, I remember that Jeremy said we are all flawed, and I wonder why some appear more flawed than others. Why sweet people can still hurt you.*

The woman my ex saw behind my back looked sweet. I saw the gentle turn of lips, the flash of guilt and understanding, as I confronted my boyfriend.

Funny, I haven't thought about her or my ex-boyfriend in years. How can I forget them so easily and yet struggle with forgetting what was done to my brother?

—ReesesCup76, The Cost of Forgiving Blog

Great, now I've sat here too long and my backside's numb.

I wiggled in the cushioned chair, gaze darting around the library. No one noticed. Well, maybe that teen in the chair nearby did; he's smirking.

Stretching my back up against the chair, I closed the laptop with one hand. With the other, I paused the music on my phone. Funny, how useful the phone is nowadays; I could probably replace my laptop with it. Nah.

Tugging out the ear buds of my headphones, I leaned over to the side and slipped them into the front pocket of my computer bag. Unzipping the main compartment, I slid in my laptop and zipped the bag up again.

I grabbed my cane; between the chilly weather and the exercises to strength my leg, the cane had become a frenemy. Once on my feet, I grabbed the bag, wishing I had stayed home as a rush of lightheadedness almost dropped me back into the chair. No, I needed more characters for my story, both physical descriptions and mannerisms. My mind already had a stockpile of plots, but plots needed players.

The library allowed me to watch people without engaging them and, with the addition of books and quiet, it was better than a mall—not that there was a mall nearby or a large store of any type really, not even a chain grocery store.

With that thought, I headed out to my truck. Whereas I used an online website for most of my groceries and other needed items, I purchased my fresh foods at the small store in town. Support local farmers, as it were. In this case, I had run out of my shampoo, as in completely gone. Not feeling like waiting the two days it took for my order to come, I planned to shop two days earlier than normal.

I found myself becoming a creature of habit, going to the store every two weeks, instead of dropping in at random times as I had done before Elijah died.

My hands tightened on the wheel as his face flashed in my mind, with lines around his full mouth and dark eyes that I had often traced with my fingertip. When he grew the beard, I complained, in jest, that the hair would hide his dimples. Oh, no, it only enhanced them.

Blinking back tears, I pulled into the tiny parking lot of the small grocery store. Withdrawing my wallet from my bag, I slipped it into my back pocket, my cell phone in the other pocket, as I got out of the truck. Slamming the door and locking it, I walked over to the front door of the store.

> *My eyes darted to the anti-aging creams lining the shelf. Was I supposed to start buying those? My reflection informed me I may have waited too long.*

Once inside, I grabbed a cart, or *buggy* as they call it here, and wheeled it down the beauty aisle. I selected my shampoo, nothing fancy, only has to be able to clean my hair thoroughly as it tended to get oily fast. Turning around, I caught my reflection in one of the hand mirrors hanging from a hook.

I so rarely looked at myself; this time, I found myself staring at a familiar stranger in the mirror.

Dad's eyes peered back at me, an electric blue that appeared kinder in his face. The shape of my eyes was like a large almond, not round like his. I had Mom's diamond-shaped face, as well as her eye shape. Funny how her face had never looked hard.

I used to loved my hair, brown with naturally contrasting shades and strands of light blonde, honey blonde, and almost black threaded throughout, different from Jeremy's and Mom's tawny hair; Dad claimed because of his early graying that he had forgotten what color hair he used to have. Mom teasingly backed him up.

Soon my hair would have strands of white or gray. Serene declared she would dye her hair pink at the first hint of graying, to her daughter's horror.

I smiled at the thought, my lips curling in the mirror. Lines deepened around my mouth and eyes. At least I know I smile more than I frown.

My eyes darted to the anti-aging creams lining the shelf. Was I supposed to start buying those? My reflection informed me I may have waited too long. Where is the timeline for when you should begin buying such things? I used facial lotion, sometimes a clay mask, and I drank lots of water. What more should I do? Stay out of the sun? I can't halt time.

I mentally shrugged and pushed my cart out of the aisle, heading for the produce. Grabbing salad items, I kicked myself for forgetting my list. Maybe check the ingredients of online recipes I was planning to try. If I had remembered to bookmark them, that is.

Pulling my cell out of my back pocket, I held it up, searching for a signal. Once the bars increased, I open the browser, which I had synched with my other devices, aka, my laptop. My tablet had broken months ago.

Yeah, I had bookmarked the recipes. Letting out a sigh of relief, I wheeled around the store, gathering ingredients. Passing the meat area, I spied a familiar lanky figure. I almost made it past before he noticed me.

"Hey neighbor," Jefferson smiled today, his face light, but his eyes wary.

"Hi. How are you?"

His brows rose, "Good, how about yourself?"

"Doing alright." Having been polite, and rather proud of myself for it, I started to wheel away, "Have a good day."

"You, too," he responded.

Nicole came over then. I hadn't noticed her standing nearby.

"Hello. Reisa, isn't it?" she said, her expression pinched.

"Yep, Reisa. Hi."

"I didn't know you shopped here." She didn't appear pleased by the fact. I noticed her uniform then, scrubs.

"Yep. Nurse?"

"What?"

"Are you a nurse?" I said, indicating her scrubs.

"Oh, yes, in fact, I am. I work over at Doctor Solomon's office."

Familiar name, how? Hmm.

"Oh, yes. The orthopedist."

"That's right," Curiosity chased some of the hostility away.

"Do you know Dr. Solomon?" Nicole inquired.

"In passing."

Jefferson, carrying something, joined us. I curled my lip at the sight of the packaged meat.

"Are you a vegetarian?" Jefferson looked amused.

"Yeah," I admitted. "You should feel judged right now. For shame." I shook my head sadly.

Joking's good. Joking is okay.

"I've wandered far from the edicts of my youth."

"Come back; we have lentils."

Jefferson laughed, "No, I still have nightmares about those. Grandma made a lentil casserole every potluck, and I had to eat it."

"It's good for you," I reminded him, "Nicole, you like lentils?"

"In soup," she brusquely answered.

"Lentil soup is rather good. I should scoot. I have ice cream in the cart. Made from milk from vegetarian cows. That makes it almost vegan."

Jefferson shook his head, "Not even close."

"Well, I draw the line at soy ice cream. Yuck. Good-bye."

"Good-bye," Jefferson replied with a smile. Nicole narrowed her eyes at me, unamused as she said good-bye.

Each interaction, as long as he understands the invisible line between us, lessens my animosity and anxiety. At least, that's what I'm telling myself. Praise Mom for instilling the ability to continue under adversary, or at least discomfort.

CHAPTER 12

Jefferson's Computer

How many pastors have I talked to over the years? This issue with forgiveness isn't new, but Elijah's death brought it back in focus. Since El died...well, the restless nights are back. I have no one to hold me, to whisper that I'm okay. Jeremy's at peace now; when he wakes, he'll be made whole.

I whisper to myself now that those who are dead will live again. It almost helps.

Why can I forgive my parents' killer, but I cannot forgive and forget what happened to Jeremy? Maybe a piece of me blames God. To me, Jeremy was like Job. Suffering after suffering brought upon his head.

He remained faithful but, unlike Job, Jeremy died.

Do I blame God for Jeremy's suffering? Am I that arrogant that I feel I can accuse God?

I already act arrogantly, withholding the forgiveness that God tells me to give.

Shame covers me.

—ReesesCup76, The Cost of Forgiving Blog

"Love is free.
It only cost your heart.
Love is unselfish.
It only demands your soul.
And Love is pure.
It only pollutes your mind."

Huh.

I sat back in the dining room chair, crossing one arm while sipping from the cup in my other hand. The poem peeked out from the screen, surrounded by comments on my forgiveness blog. My rant blog, sometimes.

Uncrossing my arm, I put the cup down on the table and my fingers on the keyboard. Beneath the poem, the poet had shared a bit of what had inspired her to write it. A boyfriend who played games with her mind, playing on her insecurities. How can she forgive him when he tore apart her heart?

Mouth twisted in sympathy, I replied as best I could. I had no aspirations of becoming an adviser. I'm stumbling through this world as well, barely holding my own light up against the darkness. Still, I can spare an insight or two, help her dodge a rock or three in the narrow path.

Enough stalling. Write.

When I finished, I shut the cover. I stood, hobbling over to the kitchen to dump out the cup.

I heard a chime, and I glanced at my phone. I did not remember changing the text tone. A knock sounded through the house.

Oh, the door.

Pulling my robe tightly around me, I walked out into the living room, then down the stairs to the front door. Cold stone greeted my bare feet before I stepped onto the small rug. Wishing I had gotten around to getting a dog, I peeked through the side window. With a grimace, I unlocked the door, allowing a blast of cold to come in.

Coat covered in bits of snow, woolen hat pulled snug over his ears, Jefferson offered me a small smile.

"Hey, sorry to bother you."

His eyes dropped down, perusing my outfit, his smile widening.

"Bathrobes and PJ's are the latest fashion craze," I noted, crossing my arms.

His eyes jumped back to mine, "Yeah. Sorry. My Internet isn't working, I do not know if it's my computer or the area is down."

"Did you check the area on your phone?" I grabbed the door with one hand, silently barring him. Come on, girl, you know you're going to let him in.

"Nathan borrowed my phone. I have a landline, but I can't seem to find the company's number. All that information is in my cell."

He bent his head, his eyes peering at me, abashed.

"I learned that lesson. Misplaced my cell, with all my contacts a year or so ago. Bad. I made up a binder with the information once I found it again." I chuckled.

"Do you have Internet access?"

"Yep."

"Shoot. That means it's my computer."

"Or you forgot to pay your bill," I offered innocently.

He ignored that, "Do you know anything about computers? I mean, I know you do, but I mean the hardware part or whatever they call it. I need to get some things submitted; I'm on a deadline," he pleaded.

My dilemma. Have him describe the issues or take the bull by the horns, saving us both frustration, and go look for myself?

I stepped away from the door, "I can look it over. Come in." I shut the door after him, leading him up the stairs.

"Would you like anything to drink?" I asked.

"No, thank you." Again, his face turned curious, "I'm sorry for invading your space."

Lifting my chin, "What can one do? I understand deadlines. I'll be right back. Make yourself comfortable."

I disappeared into my bedroom, locking the door behind me. After a quick trip into the bathroom to brush my hair, wash my face, and throw some lotion on my dry skin, I changed into some old jeans and a sweatshirt. Elijah's favorite sweatshirt, in fact, with "Keep calm and don't blink" written across the front.

Why do we call it bittersweet pain, the feeling that comes on us when we remember our loved ones? The sparks of agony have changed into embers of sorrow, but I find nothing sweet about the pain, just bitterness.

Socks on, I opened the door. Jefferson doesn't stay put very well, I noticed. He was in the hallway, looking at the photos lining the wall.

"Not a lot of personal pictures," he commented, leaning in to examine one.

"Why do I need them when I don't even have to close my eyes to see their faces? Heck, I saw Mom's face in the mirror just now."

He turned his head, "You favor your Mom?"

"I'm a larger-sized version of her in some respects, yes. She was short," With one hand hovering near my shoulder, I moved my other hand to well over my head. "Mom, Dad. I measure midway between them."

Jefferson nodded slightly, "And your brother?"

I dropped my hands to my side.

"Dad's height. Excuse me, I need to grab my bag." I brushed by him, turning into my office where I kept my bag. Jefferson filled the doorway behind me.

"Nice computer."

I glanced over at my new desktop.

"Thanks. I got a good deal on it. I needed a graphic powerhouse; my laptop wasn't cutting it."

I grabbed the bag off the floor. I should find a place for it instead of dropping it wherever I stopped once I got home.

"You're an artist."

Brilliant. The art supplies tip you off?

I bite back the comment on my tongue.

"A hobby."

He moved out into the hallway. I stepped by him, headed to the dining room to grab my laptop and cell phone, then down the stairs for my shoes.

"I can drive you over," he said as I grabbed my keys from the basket on the table by the front door.

"Nah, thanks, but I think I know the way."

I locked the door after us. He had parked next to my truck, so he followed down the stairs.

"Oh, no. I forgot my cane." I paused on the stairs.

"I've noticed you limping more," he said, before offering to grab the cane.

"Yeah, apparently I went overboard in some areas. Still, I'll make do without the cane. See you in a few minutes."

I got into the truck, leg aching because, of course, I had forgotten the painkillers this morning. Well, given my growing dependence on them, that was a good thing.

Jefferson backed out, turning his SUV to head out of my driveway. I followed him, making the turn down his driveway for the first time. The road curved through the trees. I noticed a trail on either side, then the trees cleared barely enough to allow for a cabin.

I had looked at this house online, curious about the surrounding neighborhood. Bigger than my own, parts of this log cabin-styled house dated back to the early 1900s. It sat on a hill, surrounded by mature trees. From the parking area, a staircase curved through two landings to the front porch.

I parked next to Jefferson, pausing a moment before getting out of the truck to draw a deep breath. Bag in hand, I got out, walking over to where Jefferson waited by the wooden steps.

"Stairs, sorry." Jefferson said, "You go first; take your time."

"See, I thought there would be a chairlift," I joked. "Go ahead, I feel better not having someone behind me."

Jefferson bounded up the stairs, while I followed a bit more slowly, pride stinging, just a bit. It is what it is, this thorn in the flesh. It's all cosmetic down here on earth. This too shall pass away. Still, annoying.

Jefferson unlocked his front door, pushing it open for me to pass through.

"Thank you."

Stepping inside, I took in the interior. The front door opened into a great room with a fireplace to the right, a dining room straight ahead, and a breakfast bar separating the kitchen from the rest of the house. Large windows looked out at the forest on either side of the fireplace and behind the table in the dining room. Wood gleamed from almost every surface, from the walls to the floor and even on the countertops in the kitchen.

Having forgotten my coat as well as my cane in my rush to get this over with, I felt the chill from the open door. Jefferson stood, watching me scrutinize his house.

"Nice," I said.

Along the wall running perpendicular to the door, there was a shoe rack. I took off my shoes, lining them up in front of the rack. I placed my bag near the coat rack. Moving away from the cold, into the house, I glanced at Jefferson.

"Where's the patient?"

"The patient? Oh, the computer. This way."

He took off his own boots, hanging up his coat. Walking past me, leaving me to follow him down the open doorway I saw on the left. A few open doors lined either side of the hallway, but I kept my eyes averted, not looking, not wanting to pry. The hallway ended at a small window, but Jefferson turned right. A small spiral staircase was hidden in the nook. Jefferson gave an apprehensive look at my leg.

"It's fine."

He nodded, then scaled the staircase. At the top, we emerged into a loft, the railing at one side overlooking the great room. Wooden floor up here as well, I noticed. Two bunk beds lined one wall, several small windows brought light in through the outer walls, and a rocker chair and love seat were positioned nearby. More than that, there were bookshelves. Lots of bookshelves.

"Those must have been a pain to bring up here," I commented, immediately drawn to the shelves and their contents. Books on ancient Rome, the world wars, as well as other wars, and biographies of various war heroes filled one bookshelf.

"My grandparents added this loft for the grandkids. Some friends helped them heft the furniture over the railing."

I moved to another shelf, nodding to show I had heard Jefferson. Here, on the shelf, were the photography books, with manuals on the lightroom, various cameras, techniques, and, of course, collections of photography by other artists. I found one of my favorite photographer's books on composition.

Also on this shelf were computer books, not nearly as many as photography though, as well as how- to books on various subjects. From where I stood, I eyed the other shelves, before turning my attention to the computer sandwiched between windows on the back wall. I walked over.

"Well, darling, let's see what's the problem." I raised a brow at Jefferson. "Show me where it hurts."

A smirk developed on his lips, and I regretted my joke. He joined me at the computer, punching in his password before turning it over to me. I launched his browser, reading the error message. Checking his connection, I pulled back the chair and sat down.

"It's slow," I informed him. "Do you have antivirus software?"

"I figured my raw files, my photos, were eating up too much space. I have an external hard drive to store some of my work, but perhaps I could use another one."

"Raw eats up a lot of room," I agreed, "but that isn't your problem. I do not see any protection software. That's playing with fire."

With his permission, I downloaded some software and started a scan of his computer. Should I suggest he busy himself elsewhere? I could call down the steps if I needed something, but that's tricky when you are working with someone's else's computer. So much personal information and files; I wouldn't want to leave someone alone with mine.

And yet I had left my laptop downstairs. Eying the stairs, I asked Jefferson,

"Could you grab my bag? I promise not to go through your search history."

Jefferson laughed before disappearing down the stairs. Sometimes, briefly, I forgot who he was. That's good, right?

BAM! BAM! A fist pounded on the door.

"Sheesh, hold on," Jefferson said, as the sound of the door opening resounded in the quiet house.

"I need to talk to you," interjected a female voice.

"Cole, no. I told you…."

"I know! You thought you were ready for a relationship, but you aren't. I don't believe that!"

"Cole, I'm sorry I hurt you but, really, we haven't dated that long."

I cupped my hands over my ears, humming under my breath, I hated breakups, the messy emotions. Dropping my hands, I kept humming, remembering how I wanted Jefferson to be alone and unhappy. Getting my wish wasn't very satisfying when there was another heart involved.

Their voices lowered, thankfully. Mumbled words drifted up, but I huddled near the screen of the computer, refusing to engage my ears.

Suddenly, "Whose bag are you holding?! And whose car is outside?!"

I whistled under my breath. This Cole can screech with the best of them.

"Who's here, Jeff?"

Nicole's voice increased in proximity as she threw questions at Jefferson. My gaze darted to the stairs, where first the head and then the body of Nicole appeared. She halted briefly when she saw me, her eyes puffy, her lips pulled tight.

"You." She choked.

Insert sinister laugh? That fits this role in a play I never auditioned for. I stood up.

"Hello, Nicole. Jefferson, you have my bag?" I kept my voice neutral but friendly.

Nicole finished climbing the stairs, revealing that she was wearing her scrubs, like the other day. Jefferson came up, my bag in hand.

"Why are you here? Ginger said you were a hermit or something."

"Cole," Jefferson warned.

"Well, I make an exceptions for computers." I took my bag from Jefferson. "You have some malware on your computer. It'll take a while to get rid of it."

"Malware?" Jeff made a face, "How did I get malware?"

"There are plenty of ways, from pop ups on questionable sites, for example. Hackers are quite clever nowadays with inserting their viruses. You could have simply clicked on the wrong link and, with nothing protecting it, had something downloaded to your computer."

"Never date someone your mom suggests," he lowered his voice, looking haggard. "Or a family friend. It makes it awkward when you break up."

I pulled out my laptop, "Your Internet is working fine, which is why I could download the software by the way. If you don't mind, I'm going to work on some things while waiting for the scan to run. Can I have your router information?"

"Oh, yeah, sure. I have it written down here." Jefferson grabbed a notebook off his desk, flipping through it. Nicole, shoulders hunched, waited while Jefferson read off the information.

"Okay. Thanks." I waved a dismissive hand. I pulled myself into the nearby rocker chair with a view of the desktop, bent on working on my story.

"Sorry," Nicole mumbled, leaving the loft. I glanced over to the stairs, meeting her eyes briefly. Hurt and embarrassment warred in her face. I didn't know what to say. She didn't wait anyway, averting her eyes, then disappearing down the stairs.

"You know, you could install regular stairs leading to the loft," I told Jefferson.

"Would ruin the flow of the downstairs, or so my Grandma said when they discussed the stairs. You okay if I head down?"

"I'm fine."

"I'm sorry for the drama."

"Please, life is drama." Realizing how that sounded, I added, "No apologies necessary."

That curious look appeared on his face, his mouth opened.

"Jeff?" Nicole called.

"Never date someone your mom suggests," he lowered his voice, looking haggard. "Or a family friend. It makes it awkward when you break up."

"See, my brother taught me that, along with how to hit a baseball," I answered, returning my eyes to my laptop screen.

"Good for you." Jefferson disappeared downstairs.

The mumbles of voices returned. Pulling my iPod out of the laptop bag, I put the headphones on and clicked on a playlist.

CHAPTER 13

Confrontation

Today I do not feel like writing. Today I feel like crying.

That means I need to write even more, right? Letting these emotions fester inside of me, concealing the depths of pain with quips of humor, deepens my depression. I don't want to go there again.

I spent a long, sleepless night last night, reliving the pain of those last weeks with my brother. So many days watching him suffering, praying for a respite for him. We all knew the end was waiting for him, but he held on, fought.

Until that day, after that, he let go.

I saw it, knew why he did it. He was giving her freedom to pursue her happiness, even as his heartbreak drained the last bit of strength from his fighting spirit.

Mom taught me to radiate the epitome of polite manners, of which I have failed more often than not. I had lost the ability to extract myself from a situation with grace. Luckily, my ability to feel mortified has eroded over the years.

The last time I saw her, I wanted her to suffer. I wanted her to feel the pain my brother did.

What stopped me from tearing into her was the shell she had become.

Chapter 13: Confrontation

Revenge isn't sweet; revenge doesn't heal; it doesn't undo. In some sense, I had my revenge, unsought. She accomplished that by punishing herself. Years have passed, and I faced the other player in that tragic game.

I wanted him to suffer, but that doesn't satisfy either. Does he miss her? It's been eleven years. Would I wish the same fate on him as on her? No, since I didn't want that fate for her.

Maybe that's why I have trouble forgiving. I never got a chance to rage before she was gone, too.

—ReesesCup76, The Cost of Forgiving Blog

When I came downstairs, Nicole was standing in the living room, tears on her face, screaming at Jefferson that he needed to let go, that everyone was tired of him wasting away, that he needed to live, that he needed to be happy. Of course, it was obvious that Nicole felt that happiness was to be found with her.

I tried to catch Jefferson's attention.

"She's dead! She's not coming back, and you need to move on!"

"You have no idea what you're talking about," Jefferson growled.

I felt a sting of pain from my lip as I bit down with my teeth, mixed with the fog of pain in my head. I needed to leave. This hurt to hear. Plus, his computer was clean. Short of waving my arms, I couldn't catch his eye as he argued with Nicole. I sat on the bench to put my shoes on.

"Ah, when to the heart of man
Was it ever less than a treason
To go with the drift of things,
To yield with a grace to reason,
And bow and accept the end
Of a love or a season?"[3]

I mumbled under my breath, tasting Robert Frost's words, wondering if he was right. Accepting appeared to be the sounder option. Shoes on my feet, bag hanging on my shoulder, I opened the door. I'll text Jefferson later.

---

[3] Frost, Robert. "Reluctance." "Frost Quotable Quotes." Goodreads. https://1ref.us/1sv. Accessed December 23, 2021.

"What did you say?" Nicole asked.

So close. I shut the door and turned to face the two sets of faces, one glaring, one puzzled.

"I was quoting Robert Frost."

"What did you say though?" Nicole pressed.

"Something I'm regretting now?"

Nicole scowled at me, "If you're done, we need some privacy. We all know you like your own privacy."

I flashed a huge grin at her, unperturbed, "I do. I really do. Jefferson, your computer's spotless currently. I set it up to scan every so often. Still, be careful with the websites."

> *I've learned the harder you try to hold on to something, the slipperier it becomes. Perhaps from the sweat of effort or blood leaking from the heart.*

I had reopened the door and, with my last words, I limped out and down the stairs.

"Cole! Why are you being mean to her?" I heard Jefferson yell. He had no problem catching up with me, I'm not actually setting speed records anymore.

I turned and held up one hand, "No worries, alright? Let me know if there are any more issues with your computer."

Jefferson rubbed his hand in his hair, "Thanks. I'll pay you for your time."

"No thanks. I'm just being neighborly. It can be fun."

Resuming my descent, I reached my truck, Jefferson behind me.

"Take me with you. That would be neighborly."

He was joking, mostly, but my shoulders drooped. Why is life so sad?

"I'm not giving you advise, The Father knows I tried to avoid hearing anything." I hesitated, seeing Nicole in the doorway.

Jefferson put his hands in his pockets.

"But?" he prompted.

"Don't throw away your future for your past."

"Interesting advice." He emphasized *advice* with a cynical smile.

"It would be, if I had offered it. I didn't. I'm thinking out loud. Honestly. I've learned the harder you try to hold on to something, the slipperier it becomes. Perhaps from the sweat of effort or blood leaking from the heart. Who knows? Bye!" I added.

I opened the truck door, getting inside. Shutting the door, I started the engine. Backing away, both physically and mentally from the mess, I wondered why I said anything.

Minutes later I entered my home. Discarding my things, I grabbed my medicine out of the main bathroom. Padding down the hallway, the photos on the wall grabbed my attention. There were only three, carefully selected for their low threshold of pain. In one, I stood surrounded by my parents and Jeremy, holding my baptismal certificate, hair still damp. Dad had gone to church early that day to turn on the water heater so the water was warm for me. I ran my finger above the frame, trying not to smear the glass protecting the photo. Dad looked so proud.

The second photo was taken by Jeremy's wife, with Jeremy and I beaming at the camera from a canoe. Jeremy had insisted I learn how to paddle during one camping trip, forcing me into the water. It took a while for me to get the hang of the rhythm.

The last photo, the one Jefferson had been inspecting, captured Elijah. Seated at the table, his birthday apple pie in front of him, he was frozen in time, leaning back against his chair, laughing. I loved that image, his dimples flashing, somehow capturing the air of joy around him.

Smiling slightly—for how could I not while remembering Elijah?—I continued to the kitchen for a glass of water.

After taking my pain medicine, I headed into the back room, along with my little portable speaker and iPod. After starting a fire in the little wood stove, I put on some music then pulled over the glider I keep in the room. Selecting "Playlist," I pushed "Shuffle," and then rocked gently, staring at the fire.

Elijah, he still makes me smile, Even with him gone, even with the thought of him hurting, I'm smiling.

"Ah, when to the heart of man...."[4]

Pausing the music, since my mind was already filled already with poetry, I recited the rest of the poem.

"Was it ever less than a treason
To go with the drift of things,
To yield with a grace to reason,

---

[4] Ibid.

And bow and accept the end,
Of a love or a season?"

That wasn't the whole poem, but the most quoted portion. What was it called? I couldn't remember. No, wait. "Reluctance," that's right. About autumn's end.

A treason to accept the end of a love, for love never ends, does it? Stronger than death, or so Solomon once wrote.

Hugging myself, I forced my mind down another line of thought. I needed to work on my recent tendencies to blurt out thoughts. For a time after Elijah's death, thoughts failed to form, much less words. Lee worried that I had become a mute. Look at me now, spewing advice for the broken both online and in real life.

<u>BAM, BAM, BAM!</u>

Rather glad I hadn't changed back into my PJs, I went down to answer the door.

Peeking through the side window revealed Nicole, shivering in her little coat. She saw the curtain moved and turned to look at me.

People could die from such a look.

Despite fearing for my life, I opened the door.

"Stay out of my personal business!" she blurted out, leaving me with my mouth open. I shut it, paused, then shrugged.

"Okay," I replied and started shutting the door. She reach forward to stop it from closing, pushing back. I held it firmly, my lips also in a firm line.

"That's it? Okay?"

"You came to my house, are stopping me from closing my door, and you want me to leave you alone. Okay doesn't begin to cover it, but it's nicer than what I could say."

Her mouth dropped, "You are unbelievable. You worm into Jefferson's life...."

"No." I shook my head.

"...and now you are offering him advice." She spoke over me, "What's your deal? Playing head games with him? This hard-to-get act is a bit young for you, don't you think?"

I dropped my hand, and the door swung back. She barely caught herself from falling.

"Do you have any idea how off-base you are?" Head starting to pound, I added, "I mean, who bases her opinion of someone based on two meetings, before today, with barely a hello exchanged?"

"Oh, I know all about you." She crossed her arms.

"Not from me, which mean its gossip." I fixed her with what Jeremy called my freezing stare, "You are too old to take as fact what people give as opinion. Whoever fed you information about me, whatever they told you, I don't really care."

"I've read your website." Came her defiant offense.

"The Introvert Review? *Introvert.* Meaning, *not social*," I paused, then continued, "If you can glean information about me from there, more power to you. Although, I think you could gain knowledge about a person based on the books they read and like."

I held up a hand to halt her from speaking,

"From what I recall, I do not have any man-trapping books reviewed on there. I'm tired, I'm hurting, and I've spent the last hour or so trying to stave off this headache from all the yelling you've been doing. Now, thanks to this, I've failed." Her cheeks flushed, and her gaze darted away.

"The advice I handed out and, yeah, I'll admit I handed out a piece, I regretted it instantly. Wanna know what I said?, It was very deep and profound. I said, "Do not throw away your future for your past." Someone once said it to me, and it helped. I thought, hey, why not? Now, if you will excuse me…."

"You're weird," she tossed out.

"Good gracious, do you believe if you toss enough names at me they will stick?" I slammed the door shut, locking it. I'm getting that dog, a big scary one with lots of teeth.

"You stay away from Jefferson! He doesn't need another tragic female in his life!"

Now she's yelling through the door. I released a deep-hearted sigh.

"Aunt Ellen told us all about you!" she added.

I closed my eyes and leaned my forehead against the door, fighting the chill in my bones. Ellen told her all about me? How much of that was

> *"Oh, I know all about you." She crossed her arms. "Not from me, which mean its gossip." I fixed her with what Jeremy called my freezing stare, "You are too old to take as fact what people give as opinion.*

really the truth, on Nicole's side as well as Ellen's? Stomach churning, I opened my eyes as I moved away from the door.

I needed to get my own house in order. Might as well do it now, before—well, before I lose my nerve and hide. I trusted Ellen, should have known that would bite me in the end.

Five minutes later, I opened the door again, ready to go out. Leg aching less—thank you drugs—but I still brought my cane.

Nicole, having screamed a few more choice things at my closed door, was getting into her car, which was parked behind my truck, when I appeared.

Having vented her fury, she looked defeated, and oh, so young. It seemed only the young rage against heartbreak; the old have learned to accept the way of things. Save your fight for something you can win. And one rarely wins against another person's stubbornness, I thought, remembering Jefferson's obvious annoyance while Nicole cried.

I'm not involved with this, not really. The idea of dragging another person into a breakup as Nicole attempted to do, I mean, why? Isn't that embarrassing?

She paused upon my arrival. I tossed my bag into the truck, no way I'm walking over to Ellen's, and climbed inside.

She came over to tap on the window. I stared forward for a moment, contemplating whether I should encourage further insults or not.

"Please," She said loudly.

Engine going, I rolled down the window.

Face still insolent, Nicole attempted to be apologetic. "I'm sorry. Mama always said when I start to blow up, it's best to keep away. No one can reason with me."

Several responses ran through my mind, some of which were unChristlike to say, others which invited more confidence. The last thing I wanted was to be stuck in this mess.

Whatever went across my face made Nicole pale.

"I'm sorry, okay? Do not go rushing off to tell Jefferson."

I bark a laugh, "That's what you think I'm doing? Look, I do not know what has been said to make you believe I have this relationship with Jefferson, but I do not. I'm not offering advice to you or him. The Father knows I regretted saying anything before, but let's agree I've been punished quite thoroughly. Now, I have to set my own house in order. Someone's been telling stories out of school."

"Huh?"

"Never mind." I rolled up my window. Pulling forward, backing out at an angle onto the grass, and turning my truck to head out the driveway, then I slammed on the brakes.

Jumping out of the truck, cane in hand, I cut a quick path to where Nicole stood outside her car.

"Sorry, can't do it."

"Do what?" She stammered, leaning away from me, her back pressing against the car. Where was that woman who had been screaming at me less than ten minutes ago?

I guess a woman with a cane can be intimidating.

No, honestly, I could see that. One never knows how the cane will come into play.

"Leave this alone. What exactly did Ellen tell you about me? You appear to think you have all this knowledge about me which, in all honestly, frustrated me because I've been minding my own business this last year. What do you think you know?"

Her mouth tried to work, but a flush returned to her cheeks. Oh, good, her temper's returning. Well, I have one too, and I'm tired of minding my words.

"You know, I was trying to have a sick day today. I was going to watch some movies on my laptop, catch up on some writing, maybe try out a few recipes later. What I wasn't going to do was fix the computer of a neighbor I've barely interacted with, get an earful of a breakup of a relationship I had no interest in, and get screamed at by a stranger. Because, sweetheart, I do not even know your last name, just your profession and a suspicion that you are related to Ellen. Yeah, I caught that—Aunt Ellen.

"If I had been the curious sort, looking at the family photos she had lying around, perhaps I would have seen your face smiling at me, but I'm not. Perhaps I will look today, when Ellen and I have our long overdue talk. I'll look over those photos to see whom I should avoid, because Ellen, whom I liked, for goodness sake, has been feeding people misinformation about me, and I don't like that."

I paused for breath, my heart thumping faster.

"Not at all," I quieted my voice, "Would you like it if you wanted peace so much you moved hours away from everything that once gave you joy, just to have another drama pull you in? Or back in?"

My head throbbed. I should be numb. Afraid I would snap the carved bird right off the top, I loosen my grip on the cane.

"And Jefferson. What is it about that man? Why do women lose their heads for him? He's just a man—handsome, sure—but I bet that snake in the Garden of Eden was gorgeous and look where that led Eve."

Nicole stared at me with wide eyes, her chest moving a bit rapidly.

Drawing a deep breath and releasing it slowly, I gentled my tone.

"In another life, I would sympathize with you. In another time, I would grab chocolate and let you vent. If you were my friend. If we <u>knew</u> each other. We do not. I could point out, self-righteously, that I'm not making judgments about you; you're the one who sought me out to tell me off for imagined offenses."

With a self-deprecating tone I added, "But I'm not one to act religiously. I'm not the one to say attacking another woman because she happened to be at his house—<u>working</u>—and assuming because she's a woman that she must be after your man—seems rather ridiculous, doesn't it, not to mention presumptuous. Good graces, woman, he broke up with you. Whatever reason he used, screaming at him isn't going to change his mind."

I bit off the rest of my words.

"Now that I have thoroughly ruined my calmness—goodness knows driving off without confronting you would have been the high road—but now I'm going to get into my truck and confront someone I once liked. Good day."

I marched over to my truck, slammed the door shut behind me and sped off.

CHAPTER 14

Ellen

I'm feeling rather pressed today. It's been a few days since I blogged on here, because I've been busy putting my own house in order.

Too bad my house is made of cards. Oh, how strong we think our walls are, keeping society out, until the wind blows at just the right angle to blow it all down.

Like that? That bit of prose comes after a long session of soul-searching, after confronting the wolf that blew my house down.

That was fun!

As much as I would like to keep this metaphor going, I've drawn this out long enough. Well, not really long enough, but it's slightly off the subject of the blog, which is forgiveness.

I've read so many books about forgiveness. Each piece of advice paves the correct path, yet I still find myself knee-deep in a sinkhole, having missed where the path curved.

"It is easier to forgive an enemy than to forgive a friend"[5]

Betrayal from an enemy can still catch you off guard, break your trust. An enemy can be trusted, surprisingly.

---

[5] William Blake Quotable Quote. https://1ref.us/1sw. Accessed December 24, 2021.

> *Betrayal from a friend or family member breaks more than your trust; it breaks your heart. It's more than pride that halts forgiving a friend, it's fear. Once hurt so completely, could one survive another break? They say something broken can mend and become stronger, but something broken repeatedly can lose pieces. Losing pieces of yourself and losing the shape of what you were.*
>
> *Does my rambling make sense?*
>
> —ReesesCup76, The Cost of Forgiving Blog

Can't say this was my longest emotionally draining day, but it ranked up there. A blink later and I pulled up into Ellen's parking area.

Pain radiated through my jaw, as I unclenched it. Walking here would have given me time to calm down. Turning off the engine, I sat, staring Ellen's house, trying to calm myself in the details.

Unlike mine, excluding in the back, the area around Ellen's home had been cleared of trees, creating what must appear to be a bald spot when viewed from the sky. The colonial traditional house sat on flat land, a large garden in the back as well as a playset for the grandkids. Ellen loved her flowers, and the front porch was lined with plant beds that soon would contain tulips and other early flowers. Bushes were nicely trimmed back since I was last here.

Hmm. I needed to work on my yard.

I left the truck and scaled the front porch steps. Here the sagging wood had been replaced with fresh boards, and the rails replaced.

Her kids had been busy.

Opening the screen door, I knocked on the steel-reinforced door, then stepped back to allow the screen door to shut.

A flutter of movement in the long panel by the side of the door, then Ellen appeared behind the screen. She pushed open the screen door as well, her face slightly flushed.

"Reisa. Come in."

I hesitated.

Ellen waved in me, still holding the screen. "Come on, it is chilly out."

I passed her, and she shut both doors then stepped around me.

"Come, take off your coat."

"I can't stay long."

"Well, have some tea at least."

She disappeared toward the kitchen.

Catching a flash of light, I stared into the mirror in the foyer, positioned over a side table. It revealed a woman with her braid slightly undone, eyes glittering, cheeks reddened from the cold. Lines deepened around the woman's mouth.

I looked so tired, wearing my mother's face of bone weariness. Sometimes even saints were worn out by the sheep, and I would see the fringes of Mom's patience. I looked like her now.

Sorrow took hold of anger, dulling the edges.

The foyer turned into a hallway, an open archway on my left leading to a living room with a large fireplace, family room on the left, with built-in shelving. I passed the stairway along the left wall, the hallway narrowing as I walked by another door, the bathroom situated under the stairs, another door leading into the formal dining room on the right, approachable by the living room as well, and finally reaching the kitchen entrance on the right at the end of the hallway.

Ellen busied herself preparing the tea, setting a plate of cookies on the small table in the kitchen.

"Help yourself, sweetie."

I seated myself at the table, limbs heavier than when I had left my home. Reaching out, I grabbed a sugar cookie and took a bite. My stomach rolled, reminding me I hadn't eaten since breakfast. The pain medicine was having a field day with my stomach.

I grabbed a napkin from the little pile on the table, setting my cookie on it. By unspoken assent, Ellen and I didn't speak until the tea was on the table, and she was seated across from me.

"Nicole—I do not know what her last name is—she swung by today," I said after a sip of the herbal tea, "It appears she believes she knows me very well, you know, for a woman who had only met me twice before today."

Ellen looked embarrassed, "She's my niece. My husband's youngest sister's child. Her father's from Chile or one of those countries down there."

"Interesting."

Ellen flinched slightly at my dry tone.

"You've been avoiding me," I flinched myself at the accusation in my voice. "A two-way street, honestly. So, how do these people—for Jefferson and his family seem to feel they know me as well—how do these people have this information?"

"You shouldn't have made friends with me," Ellen surprised me by responding. "I can't keep my mouth shut. Marcus often complained about it."

I noted she had put the burden on me, I shouldn't have befriended her. She appeared chagrinned, but there was a challenge as well in her eyes.

Of course, my fault. I liked her. I liked the visiting over tea, I liked the discussions on various house designs. She had been an architect before retiring. She and her late husband had had their own business, with her husband working the construction side. I took the gossiping in stride. We all have our cherished sins. I believed, at one point, that I hadn't fed her addiction. But gossip addicts are clever; they can pick up pieces of information and paste them together.

I folded my arms on the table, bracing myself, as she continued.

"Jefferson such a good boy, really, and he's been alone so long. Such a good Christian boy. When Nathan started acting out, Ginger told me Jefferson took him aside, had a good talk with him. Slowed that flirty boy down, about all one could do really. Nathan's such a charmer."

"Hmm, seems like you know them well."

Ellen looked away, abashed. "I may have fibbed a bit about Jefferson. He does keep to himself."

"But you do talk to him, more than you said."

Not that I cared, really.

"Yes," she admitted. "At first, I didn't know if you were looking, so to speak."

I shook my head. "You hinted, strongly, that I should meet Jefferson."

"I did." She folded her hands on the table, gazing at them, "Testing you. I would have warned Jefferson if you had been interested," She gave a small shrug, peeking up at me, "I have done that before."

I detected pride in her voice. I couldn't fathom why. Each must fight his or her own battles. I had no one fighting mine, to be left alone.

"You are such a sweet girl," she said, breaking into my musing about large guard dogs. "I realized almost instantly you were exactly the type of girl Jefferson needed, a quiet soul like him. You are quite beautiful, you know. I can understand the limp making you doubt yourself, but you are quite active, hiking and all. Jefferson wouldn't mind the limp."

How could I not see Ellen clearly? Her words twisted my stomach, then appealed to my vanity.

"I have no issue with my looks, Ellen." I spoke low.

"And you shouldn't! That's what I'm saying!" Ellen perked up, her eyes gleaming, "That pretty hair and skin. Jefferson even mentioned how pretty you were to Ginger."

Oh, great.

"Did he now?"

"Oh, do not be embarrassed." She patted my hand, mistaking my look, "Now, I know Jefferson was seeing Nicole, and they were quite nice together, but there are other…." She paused, seeing me shaking my head. "Sweetheart, if you had been a bit nicer on Christmas to Ginger and her family, you could have been with Jefferson. It's too late now; Nicole told me they were quite happy."

"Oh, did she now?" I would have laughed, if it wasn't so sad. I drew a steadying breath. "Look, I don't want to date Jefferson or anyone…."

Ellen interrupted, "Man isn't meant to be alone."

"So, are you dating then?" I inquired.

"Of course not!" She said, indignantly.

"Doesn't Paul say it would be better if we were all like him? If you feel I should ignore that advise, why aren't you?"

"I had a good man and a good marriage," she informed me. "I do not need to remarry."

I smiled softly, knowing I was about to feed her addiction.

"So did I."

"You're a widow?" Ellen pulled back in her chair, astonished. I don't know if she knew she had increased the space between us, without leaving her chair. "I didn't know."

"What do you know?" I queried. "It appears you have more details than I was aware of. Nicole gave me some choice opinions."

I watched the war playing across her face, debating what to ask about first, my marriage or Nicole.

Family won.

"Nicole's a nice gal." Her voice held a question.

"Nicole's rather hurt right now. If you two are tight, you may want to call her." I stood up, "I came here determined to settle the issues between us. I do not like the atmosphere between us at church, and I really do not like hearing opinions about myself being given as fact. What have you been saying to people, Ellen?"

Ellen planted a hand on her chest, "Me? Only good things! I mean, I may have mentioned that you never seem to go anywhere, how no one seems to come to visit. You can be rather taciturn around others. I mean, I would see you regularly, but then you would disappear for a while in that house. You have so few photos of yourself and of your family. I figured you had an unhappy childhood. Then there are no photos of friends. Well, there's that one…." Light dawned on her face, "Oh my gracious, that man who is laughing, that was your husband, wasn't it?" I remained mute. "It was! I saw the other one, the one with you with a man in the canoe, but you two looked alike. I figured a brother or cousin."

I had overlooked the essence of this woman. Her desire to spin opinions as facts, with the hint of malice, made up more of her personality than I had accounted for.

"Jefferson's a good man, isn't he?"

Blinking at my non sequitur, she still nodded eagerly, "Yes, he is."

"And Nicole's a nice girl." No question in my voice this time, "It seems that you, who are so eager to know everything about everyone, don't know those two so well."

She rose, indignant, "How dare you."

Seeing Ellen's intelligence, I had overlooked the essence of this woman. Her desire to spin opinions as facts, with the hint of malice, made up more of her personality than I had accounted for. I had chosen poorly. That fact discouraged me. I liked observing people, identifying different personalities. I thought I had figured out whom to stay away from. I guess not. The price of arrogance, of thinking I, along with God, could see into the heart.

"I don't care what lies you've been spreading at this point. Gauging by those who have accepted your word without question, I wouldn't want to befriend them anyway. I'll show myself the way out."

Ellen's heeled shoes tapped down the hall after me.

"What did you do to Nicole." She demanded, as she stood on the porch and I was halfway to my car.

"Nothing. Jefferson, however, broke her heart. Or her pride. It was hard to gauge which with her screaming at me. Apparently you believed I was interested in Jefferson," I said while my hand rested on the truck door handle.

Ellen didn't reply, her body stiff.

"You should have tried your hand at fiction. This story you wove around me would have had a decent chance of selling. You know, injured woman with loner tendencies, moving to the countryside to avoid love. Then one day she meets a handsome, yet emotionally wounded, neighbor. They are so alike, but, oh, the woman's insecurities, about her injury and her looks, stop her from entering into a relationship. When will she realize how lonely she really is before it's too late? Of course, there's the encouraging neighbor, friend to both and, yes, the obligatory beautiful female also interested in our hero."

I made a face as I paused, reflecting.

"Not my cup of tea, so to speak, but a nice story. May even have been true for some other woman, in some other place. Me, I do not make a good heroine, and I do not fit your story. Permanently lame, trust me, my leg isn't a thing of beauty, but as for low self-esteem," I shrugged. "Mom used to warn of the dangers of being too fond of one's own reflection. Whether thinking oneself pretty or ugly, one can become so obsessed as to forget the temporary nature of the body. Perception colors our eyes anyway, doesn't it? Can you really say with certainty that everyone will find a particular person beautiful?

"As for my relationship, I have loved deeply and have been loved deeply. A real marriage full of disagreements, friendship and, yes, passion; I miss him every day. Was that tragic, losing him?" I fought the lump in my throat. "Yes. The love story you carved out for me has already occurred, complete with an heroic sacrifice. Some may want to marry again, so it's not my place to judge right or wrong. For me, I do not. I do have friends, living, breathing friends who understand my <u>need</u> for solitude."

I forced a large smile on my face, "There. That's enough fodder for gossip!"

Suddenly I jumped, seeing a man watching us from the path that ran along the front porch to the side of the house.

Jefferson uncrossed his arms, "Sorry. Didn't want to interrupt."

"Well, I'm done." I climbed into the truck, "My throat's sore from talking. I've surpassed my quota for the week."

I slammed the door shut, started the truck, and backed out of the driveway. Never once did I look at either one of them again.

CHAPTER 15

Hallway Photos

Men can change into demons, ripping at each other's emotional flesh. I should write mankind, for women are included in this. How sad that those in the image of God can be twisted into such a tragic state. Stealing what's most precious to another, as in the prophet Nathan's tale of the rich man taking the lamb from the poor man. That keeps popping up in my mind when I try to work through forgiving and forgetting. The similarities between this sad tale and that of David and Bathsheba.

Just without the remorse of David, the king.

Or perhaps there was. There were whispers of his depression.

It's coming to a point I must acknowledge that I may only be able to forgive by confronting the offender. The one still living. In forgiving him, perhaps I will forgive her.

Sometimes I read her letter and wonder if I should show it to him. That would end in confrontation as well.

It's interesting that I'm sharing this with you, my readers. How confusing my language must appear at times, as I attempt to avoid using too many names. Nothing in this world can be truly anonymous. There's enough paranoia in me to avoid giving too many details, in the rare chance that he might see this blog and recognize the players.

> *Yet there's nothing new under the sun. One betrayal may mimic others before and foreshadow those after.*
> *My struggle to release my anger has played out over time as well.*
> —ReesesCup76, The Cost of not Forgiving Blog

March blew into April; I attended church faithfully, expecting at least a few cold shoulders. After all, didn't I tell off one of their own? But I had underestimated the people of the church. Sure, I received one or two looks from narrowed eyes, but most were content to accept me based on how I acted toward them, not what others said. I resisted Sabbath dinners, for the most part but, in the spirit of friendliness, I occasionally stayed for pot lucks.

People exhausted me; paradoxically, there was something inside me needing social interaction. I considered pulling up roots and going to live with Selene. The photos Selene shared, via text and Facebook, made me miss her and precious Eleni, the daughter of her heart.

There were more photos in my hallway now. I had selected a few with Lee and Selene, as well as those with some blogger friends. I couldn't bring myself yet to hang photos of Jeremy and his wife, putting up some of Jeremy and my parents instead. Elijah and my wedding photo hung in my bedroom, where I could gaze at it, cry, and remember. Remembering that day was good, it had been the second time light had returned to my life, the first being when I met Elijah.

I worked, read, and painted. Some days I even managed to hike and snap photos. My leg ached less, since I succumbed to pressure from my friends and had sought out a doctor, selecting one a decent distance from where I lived. She set up a pain management program and discussed the possibility of surgery, each of us pretending that a solution existed.

Contentment lured me into setting aside the growing conviction that eventually I needed to take action so I could let go and forgive. I reminded myself, weakly, that it wasn't a betrayal against me. Why did the inability to forgive burden me then?

Round and round I went, compelled, while getting sick of the spinning.

CHAPTER 16

Friendship

I rarely quote on this blog (well, not usually), despite the vast amount of applicable quotes. Writing someone else's words here feels a bit like borrowing someone else's legs to complete a journey. Rather revolting in thought, scratch that. Maybe saying someone else's shoes would be better. Some days, however, I find the perfect quote, one that fits my emotions that day, and I have to use it.

Did I ever mention my rule that I cannot erase what I have written, just correct misspelled words? That clears up a few things, doesn't it?

Anyway, here's the quote:

"I can forgive, but I cannot forget, is only another way of saying, I will not forgive. Forgiveness ought to be like a canceled note—torn in two, and burned up, so that it never can be shown against one."[6] Forgetting, people; it comes down to forgetting. Round and round I go, remember? Need this merry-go-round to slow down, so I can jump off.

—ReesesCup76, The Cost of Forgiving Blog

---

[6] Beecher, Henry Ward. BrainyQuote. https://1ref.us/1sx. Accessed December 26, 2021.

The droplets fell off the tree, hitting my skin with darts of coldness. I smiled; despite the chill, the forest seemed greener with the sparkling of the sun on the water. With a year and some having passed, I had observed all four seasons and their effects on the forest, and this spring weather fit my mind today. Rather corny to think so, but I'm coming to life again.

Humming an old Amy Grant song, *Ask Me*,[7] I softly sang the chorus.

River paused on the trail, her ears perked, as her mouth parted in a dog grin.

"Oh, don't laugh," I scolded, "Let's see you sing!"

River barked, making her golden fur shake.

"Now, I didn't mean it...."

River rushed by me, tail wagging. I turned around to see my guard dog enthusiastically greeting someone who, for all she knew, could be a serial killer.

"River, come."

River, with a longing look at her new friend, came to me.

"Sit."

Her furry bottom hit the trail floor.

"Stay. We've talked about this," I grumbled. "You are supposed to guard me, not make friends."

Big brown eyes gazed adoringly up at me, my hand coming out unbidden to stroke her head.

"You shouldn't have picked a golden retriever then." There was Jefferson grinning at me, walking over to my dog.

"She's a mix," I replied.

"Not one of those designer dogs?" His lip curled.

"No, not that there's anything wrong with those," I laughed, "No, River's a result of forbidden love. A purebred retriever and a dog of questionable ancestry. She favors her mom."

River's tail thumped on the ground. With a sigh, I released her and she renewed her new love affair, with me following behind.

"She's a sweetheart," Jefferson dropped to his haunches, rubbing River's head.

"She is. A decent warning system. I know someone's coming by her excitement. She's eager to greet, not defend." I smiled despite the annoyance.

---

[7] Grant, Amy, "Ask Me." *Heart in Motion*. Apple Music, ©1991.

"A German shepherd would have been better."

I gasp, reaching over to cover River's floppy ears, "Bite your tongue; she's perfect."

Jefferson laughed, standing back up.

I hooked the leash back on River's harness.

"What's her name?"

"River Song, but she goes by River."

"Riversong?"

"No, River Song. From the Doctor Who series. Her old owners called her Snowball." I exchanged a puzzle look with my dog, "We did not get it."

"Doctor Who," Jefferson inspected my shirt with its Doctor Who graphic. His eyes then continued down to my battered jeans and hiking boots before returning to my face.

Drawing a deep breath, "Well, good...."

"No, no rushing off. Please." He added, "I've been wanting to talk to you. With how the last few months have played out, but I figured I'd wait until we ran into each other."

A wave of apprehension licked at my mind. "Why?"

"Can we talk somewhere else? The cafe in town wouldn't be exactly private, everyone minds everyone else's business there, but if that would make you more comfortable...." His voice drifted off, "I realized how uncomfortable I'd been making you."

"Life's not supposed to be comfortable," I replied, wrinkling my nose, "Well, that sounds bleak. We can go to my house, I was heading back anyhow. Almost time for River's nap," I patted her head, "Lazy dog."

We made our way to my house, Jefferson quiet, me wondering what this was about.

Opening the back door, I grabbed the towel off the hook next to the coats. I cleaned off River's paws with the towel, hung it back up, then allowed her to enter. River trotted to her water dish.

Jefferson wiped his feet on the welcome mat I had placed at the back door, before entering as well. I knelt down, undid my boots. Taking them off, I lined them up under the coats.

"Want a drink?"

Jefferson was taking off his coat, "Yes, water please." He removed his shoes as well. I debated protesting the need to, but instead went into the kitchen.

Sebastian came in and wound around my legs. River gave the cat a sniff before walking to her bed in the living room and lying down.

"A cat also?" Jefferson said, surprised.

"Yeah, he's a Maine Coon. A friend brought him for me for my birthday."

Shutting my mouth to stop the flood of information, I handed Jefferson his glass of water.

"What's his name?"

"Sebastian."

Jefferson chuckled, "Sebastian?"

"Yeah, Selene brought him from a breeder who was retiring him. I tried to change his name, he refused."

Reaching down, I scooped up the cat. Sebastian started purring, the big softy.

> *So, can we try for friendship? I've honestly never asked someone that before.*

"End of March, the twenty-fifth. Let's sit in the living room." I sat on the chair, Sebastian, jumping out of my arms, sauntered down the hallway. In the living room, I noticed Jefferson staring at the photo I had added to the wall since he had last entered my home. Hanging over the couch, the large photo showed a mist rising over a small lake, infused with the colors of early morning. A woman stood on the bank, cast in shadows from the trees, staring out onto the water.

It was the only photo of her I could bear to hang up, the serenity of the frozen moment impossible to resist.

"Did you take this?"

"No, my brother did." As always, the tingle of anger nagged at my heart, "What did you want to discuss?"

"You always change the subject away from your brother."

"You want to discuss him? Funny, I didn't think you knew him." I fought the sneer from appearing on my face. If he had known Jeremy, would he have been able to do what he did?

No, Vivian had everything compartmentalized, no overlapping.

River lifted her head. It had been love at first sight for us, River and I, no extended period of bonding needed. I was her human from the first. She rose, trotting over to me, laying her silken head on my lap.

I have blessings.

Jefferson dropped to the couch, running his hand through his hair. "You know, looking back over my behavior since November—well, ever since you moved in—I'm not surprised you are so guarded with me. How arrogant I've been. Single woman moves next door, of course she's going to pursue me…."

"You're kidding me."

His face reddened, "Let me finish, please."

"Okay."

"Well, when you didn't, um, show interest, it caught my attention. That's when I lost my common sense and asked Ellen about you. That's embarrassing to admit, in light of what I overheard. Let's just say you hit pretty close to the image she was projecting. You won't ask and probably don't care," he grimaced, "but you were the first woman in years who interested me. When Ellen said you had been hurt, you needed time, I just didn't want the baggage."

He gave a cynical laugh, "Me. Like I'm such a catch, just ask Nicole."

River, sensing the tension had drained, went back to her bed to sleep.

"Not going to," I mumbled. "I'm staying far away from that one."

Jefferson's cheeks flushed, "You got an earful, I heard. I'm sorry, I didn't know she would go after you."

"Her actions were by choice; she's no puppet."

Jefferson's face sharpened, "I like you. I'm not ready for a relationship, this thing with Nicole proved that. I dated her assuming I must be. No, I just want to be friends."

"Friends?" I said in disbelief.

"Friends. It goes against pride, macho or not, to ask for friendship. I'm not lacking friends, either, but you interest me."

That surprised a laugh, "Um, thanks? I'm not too sure I'm flattered."

Jefferson bowed his head, talking to his hands, "A man and woman can be friends."

"Of course. I have plenty of male friends."

His head jerked up in surprise.

"Oh, come on. Ellen may paint me as someone with no friends, but how would she know? I mean, really, because she's known me for how long? It's ridiculous to gauge someone by the number of friends anyhow, but that's a topic for another day."

Jefferson looked sheepish. "Right. So, can we try for friendship? I've honestly never asked someone that before."

Time to reflect had shown me I didn't want to be his enemy. If I had, I wouldn't have acted as I had toward him. Helping him, finding myself joking with him. Drawing a deep breath, I nodded.

"This is unusual for me as well. Friendships are something that develop between people. I haven't selected someone and said, 'You, you are my friend.'" I shrugged, "Let's see how this goes. You may discover I'm not the fascinating person Ellen painted me as. With a limp," I added.

"Alright," he puffed up his cheeks then slowly blew out air, "This is a tad awkward."

"You're the one who finds me interesting." I shrugged. "This is me, sitting and watching the dog sleep."

We both looked over at River, who whined in her sleep.

"Why a dog?"

"I love animals," I replied. "This last year without a pet has been hard."

"I keep meaning to get another cat. Sam, my cat, died two years ago. I had him eighteen years."

"Pretty long time," I commented, giving him a sympathetic smile, "Still hard to let go. Whether it's been a long or short amount of time." Debating first, I offered, "Knight, our dog, died three years ago. I gave my cat, Stormy, to a friend when I moved. She didn't like change, and I wasn't sure how she would handle the chaos of the move. That's another reason Selene brought Sebastian. She didn't want to give Stormy back; her daughter was too attached. Like I could take anyone or anything from Eleni," I scoffed.

"Stormy and Knight?" He grinned.

"We adopted them at the same time." I smiled softly, "Elijah named them."

"Elijah, your husband."

"Yeah, my husband."

Jefferson stood up, "I need to go, things to do, people to shoot—you know, photograph." He smiled at me.

"You do portraits as well?" I stood, too.

"Not exactly, more like this." He nodded toward lake photo, "Posed, but with no emphasis on the model."

"You do nice work." Sincere, I added, "I may buy a piece of your art sometime."

"Let me know which one you like."

River's eyes opened as Jefferson hunched over to pat her.

"She's a sloth," I teased, as River closed her eyes again, "One walk and she's out."

River's tail wagged slightly.

Jefferson went back to pick up his glass of water off the coffee table. I took it from him, dropping it off in the kitchen before joining him at the back door.

"I should get a bench in here," I looked around. "Somewhere I can sit and put on my shoes."

Jefferson knelt to lace up his boots, "I have a friend who makes wooden furniture as a hobby. His carved benches are quite good."

Finished, he stood back up, "You go to church with him. Obadiah Richards."

I nodded, "Yes. I taught his son Eric in Teens. Nice kid, Eric." Amused, I added, "Based on the stuff he draws on the church bulletin when he gets bored, he's quite the budding artist."

"Yeah, restless, but a good kid."

Jefferson pulled on his coat, and I opened the door for him.

"Later," he said, stepping outside.

"Good-bye."

I shut the door after him. No one had ever asked to be my friend, except when I was a kid. The whole situation appeared clumsy and surreal, and in line with my recent realization. Was this God's hand or Satan's game?

CHAPTER 17

Lee, Andy, and Eliana

I've been thinking about a sad tale that played out at one of my father's churches when I was a teenager.

Mom once told me I had a suspicious nature, which may have led me to attribute sin to innocent blood. I loved how my mom spoke sometimes. Off subject. What opinions I voiced to her I do not remember. Sometimes I would weave stories out of hints dropped by people's behavior and, when I told my mom with a disclaimer that it was fiction, she feared my stories would fuel gossip. So she would do the parental thing and warn me off what she saw as dangerous ground. So when I noticed the following, I kept my mouth shut. At this church there was a young woman. She had been raised in an abusive home but taken out of it when she was sixteen. There were other issues, issues not shared with a fifteen-year-old, and one of the church members served as her case worker. She helped the girl get her GED, get into college, and guided the girl to the church. When my parents came to pastor the church, the girl had matured into a lovely woman. Thick honey blonde hair, big brown eyes, and a slim build—she caught my eye during a time when I struggled with my own looks. Fifteen was a rough time for me, physically. Skin and weight problems. I hit my final growth spurt, and skin cleared up. I'm fine now, thanks. Belle—not her real name—apparently had formed a friendship with her previous social worker's family. Jane, the social worker, was married to Paul, and they had a teenage son, who attended academy. The couple was in their forties when I knew them, Paul being older than Jane. Their son was Matt. Again, not real names. Belle, having finished one degree and working on a master's in child education, volunteered at an outreach organization for at risk youths. As did Jane and her husband Paul, with Jane spending less time than Paul. One Sabbath, Paul gave a talk about the organization and it successes. Belle stood beside, giving her own testimony. She also praised Paul for his hard work with the youth. Nice, sweet, but it caught my interest. I noticed, over time, how often Belle would seek out Paul at church, her constant praises bordered on hero worship. One time I was in the parents' room, watching a toddler so his mother could enjoy the church service in the sanctuary. No, not nice of me, because Mom had asked me to. Anyway, Belle came in, walked up to window, looking around the sanctuary. Her face lit up, and she fluffed her hair before leaving the parents' room. Curious, I watched her reappear inside the sanctuary, sliding next to Paul in the pew. Jane was in the kitchen with Mom prepping for pot luck, while her husband sat next to a pretty young woman. I didn't say a word to Mom, but churches are full of watching eyes. I know propriety dominates, remembering my own brush as a preteen girl hugging a grandfather figure. There had been a period when Belle and Paul's closeness had been overlooked, given Belle's history with the family. But I hadn't been alone in that parents' room; other eyes observed Belle's actions. Soon, pitying looks were sent Jane's way, knowing glances toward Paul. Someone, after witnessing more suspicious behavior than myself, came to Dad about it. Dad didn't tell me, of course. I knew because sometimes teenagers blend into the background, and so when, he asked Mom—who would not talk about it to anyone else—if she had seen anything, I was in the living room. Mom hadn't. Dad did talk to Paul, who denied anything. It was awkward for Dad, who hated any suggestion of gossip. I hated the whole thing because I liked Jane. She sometimes sought me out to visit with me after church, and I had been at her house to see her horses.

Dad and Mom retired and started attending another church, but gossip makes its way through the grapevine. Later, we heard that, during Matt's holiday break, he came home to find Paul and Belle together, kissing in the kitchen. Jane and Paul were in counseling, and Belle had stopped attending the church. That song, "Slow Fade" by Casting Crowns[8]—when I can bear to hear it—reminds me of Paul. At what point did he take that second glance? What point did Jeremy's wife?

—ReesesCup76, The Cost of Forgiving Blog

"How's that friendship thing working out?" Lee asked, a frown creasing the forehead of her regal face, her square jaw taunt, "I don't think it's going to work. Oh...give me one second."

She disappeared for a brief moment from the small Skype box opened on my laptop screen, returning with a chubby-cheeked, wide-eyed angel.

"Hello, sweetie," I cooed, leaning forward in my chair toward the laptop on the dining room table.

Securely held in her mother's lap, Eliana stared at the screen, her mouth in an "o" shape, as the most adorable noises came out of my computer. I mimicked the noises, my smile huge, as she started kicking.

"Shall I leave you two to talk?" Lee asked, humor glinting in her face.

"Will you? This is a private conversation. Isn't it Ana?"

Arms flinging as well, Ana increased the volume of her voice.

"Sleep still the main focus?" I asked, my fingers itching to touch that little face.

"What sleep? The websites say she's going through sleep regression. Selene, who you know has been through this before, laughs at me. She says fancy explanations may make new parents feel better, but they don't change a thing." Lee grumbled, "I'm so tired."

---

[8] Hall, Mark. "Slow Fade." Casting Crowns. 2007.

"I can only imagine," I sympathized, watching the hyper little princess wiggling, blue eyes bright. Those same eyes in her mother's face were puffy with bags.

"I sound ungrateful," Lee worried, "I'm not; I'm really not."

Watching Lee unconsciously stoke her daughter's arm with her thumb as she held Ana in place, I shook my head.

"No, you adore her. It shows. Do not think for a moment that being frustrated means you do not love her. Two vastly different things."

A hairy arm appeared in front of the webcam, blocking the lovely view.

"You keeping a bear as a nanny? Look at all that fur—oh, hi Andy."

"Ha, ha," I heard, as the arm disappeared with the princess. Lee tilted her face, Andy's smooth face appeared, kissing Lee soundly.

"Bye Rei."

"Bye Andy."

Lee watched them leave, stage right, before returning her eyes to me.

"What happened to the beard? I thought it looked rather charming on him."

"Church members," Lee made a face. "For some reason, they thought it looked unkempt. Andy wasn't attached to it, so he shaved it off."

"Not setting a good precedent," I warned.

"Please. There's no sense resisting on little issues."

"Hmm."

Lee's frown returned, "So, the friendship?"

I blew out a long breath before I answered, "It's going alright. It's more of a pass-each-other-on-the-trail-and-chat-for-a-few-minutes type of thing. An acquaintanceship."

"How's that feel?"

Considering my answer first, I replied, "Some days, it feels right, you know? This is real life, not a show or a book. Real life means you must move on; there's no getting revenge then fading to black or reaching the end. It's coming up on twelve years, you know."

I blinked at the sudden wetness in my eyes.

"Oh, honey." Lee sighed, "I'm coming out there. Or better yet, come out here, if just for a week."

I wiped at my eyes, "No. No. As much as I would love to with Ana getting so big, I value my sleep."

Startled, it took Lee a second, but she laughed, "Oh, you brat!"

"Be nice," my smile trembled slightly, "I'll be fine, it's just so much, ya know? Last year, too. Having Jefferson nearby brings her to mind and, with the anniversary of Jeremy's death and Elijah's less than a week after, I remember her. I mean, it's a struggle, you know? Do I even have the right to forgive? The sin wasn't against me."

"We've been over this," Lee reminded me, "She hurt you, too. She USED you. Plus, Jeremy and you were so close, what hurt him hurt you and vice versa. Remember how he acted after that boy dumped you? You hurt so much, but he was tearing up as well. That was so sweet," Lee's face gentled, "You have the right to your anger. If David and Jonathan had been born siblings, and one had been a girl, that was you and Jeremy."

"I know; I miss him too." Lee started crying as well, "He never judged me. Even when he disapproved, he treated me as a sister. The talks we had, when I wanted to rage at God, how well he listened."

"God used Jeremy to plant a seed in your heart, Andy helped it grow."

"Yeah," Lee wiped at her own eyes, "the forgiveness, how's that going?"

"Forgetting, I keep getting hung up on the forgetting. I should give him the letter," I said, "Let's see what type of man he is once he realizes I know his sin."

"Do you like Jefferson?"

"Yeah," I admitted, "He's funny, surprisingly, when he's not being pushy. We talk some about photography, but also books. He prefers nonfiction, but his brother Nathan convinced him to read some Terry Pratchett books."

Lee shook her head, "Not good."

"What?"

"Giving him the letter before he leaves your life hurts too."

That gave me brief pause, "I didn't think about that. I assumed he would go away, of course. I wanted to see him as a man, not this evil figure in my head, in case that made the whole thing easier to forgive."

"Think about it," Lee said.

"I will. Love you."

"Love you, too." Lee blew a kiss at the screen.

Shutting down Skype, I sat a moment. How was it that that had not occurred to me? That I might end up seeing Jefferson as a friend, not merely liking him in a distracted fashion. Should have thought about that before accepting the friendship, I admonished myself. That kinda leads to friendship, agreeing to be friends.

My mind tried to figure out the mess it had made. In trying to humanize Jefferson, I accepted his friendship, although I knew he probably wouldn't want anything to do with me after what I had to say.

Putting the cart before the horse, I do not see him as a friend, not yet. I should act first.

CHAPTER 18

Books

It was pointed out to me that I had shared a story without worrying if someone would recognize the tale, while I still haven't shared the details of the betrayal that launched this blog because I worried someone surfing the net would figure out the players.

You made a very good point, anonymous commenter. In this vast cyber world, the chances of the one person I want to avoid discussing this with stumbling upon this blog are slim.

The tale of Belle, Paul, and Jane was sad. The tale that still rips at my heart wasn't witnessed as a bystander, but as a person invested with two of the people. I saw the person I loved more deeply than David loved Jonathan, wounded when he was already suffering.

Not to belittle Jane's pain, I can't do that. The Jane I knew offered a smile and conversation to an awkward teen. Even if she had been stern and judgmental, I wouldn't wish what happened on her.

My story, I'm going to confront the person I've been dancing around forgiving and give him that letter. I'll share what happened after that.

—ReesesCup76, The Cost of Forgiving Blog

Spring meant I need to figure out that garden in the back. Do not want the deer that feed on it going hungry, do we?

Asking around at church led to Mr. Davis showing up with his rototiller the day after my talk with Lee. By afternoon, I had freshly turned soil but no idea what to do with it. Much research about gardening, e.g., the types of vegetables suitable for the climate and techniques for successful growing, failed to prepare me for the reality.

Gardening didn't scare me, the memory of helping Jeremy in his little box garden did. Starting the garden on the anniversary of Jeremy's death wasn't the wisest idea, in retrospect.

Setting aside my emotions, in a nice little box like Pandora's, I went to work planting broccoli, carrots, cauliflower, and other veggies. Some I had brought already started; others I planned to start from seeds. Mr. Davis warned me about the deer, advising me on the various ways to keep them at bay.

I listened politely, even inquiring about the methods, despite having read all this already on my computer. Honestly, sometimes you learn more from a person than a screen. Once Mr. Davis had left and I had planted my garden, I went inside for some iced tea.

River, rather disgruntled that I had kept her inside while Mr. Davis worked, forgave me the moment I gave her some food. Sebastian, tail weaving back and forth, appeared around the corner with a chirp meow, and I scooped him up as I passed. Sebastian purred, enjoying my caress, despite my grubby attire. In the bedroom, I deposited Sebastian on the bed, after a few minutes of loving, before heading into the bathroom.

I emerged ten minutes later, towel wrapped around myself, as Sebastian sat primly on the bed watching me retrieve my clothes. There's something unnerving about a cat watching you dress. River had joined us at this point, but she had the manners to avert her eyes.

Dressed, but with my hair still wet, I padded to my office with my little entourage, sitting down to work. The action of sitting reminded me that I had forgotten my medicine. With a sigh, I went to the kitchen. As I swallowed the pills, washing them down with some water, I noticed an approaching figure coming out from the woods.

Jefferson stopped by my new garden, inspecting it, before continuing to the house. River rushed to the back door, her tail wagging, before Jefferson could even knock.

I let him in, holding River so Jefferson could remove his shoes.

"You have a garden." Jefferson stated.

"Yes, Mr. Davis, from church, tilled the soil for me this morning. I thought why not feed the deer, ya know?"

Releasing River, she bounced around Jefferson, who bent down to pat her. I walked past Jefferson to the kitchen, offering him a drink. A pattern had developed since our truce, with Jefferson dropping by and chatting. I should have mentioned that to Lee.

Not good, Reisa girl.

Jefferson turned down the drink, and left River to greet Sebastian.

"You need to find friendlier pets," Jefferson smiled, as he rubbed Sebastian around the ears.

"Yeah, but what's a person to do?"

Jefferson turned his attention to me, "I can't stay long. You mentioned having that book of quotable quotes."

"Yes," I gestured for him to follow me as I went into the living room then down the hallway. Opening the door to the third bedroom, my office being the second, I stepped inside.

Jefferson's eyes widened as he stood in the doorway, "Wow." He walked into the room, looking over the bookshelves. "You have a lot of books."

Books filled the walls, with a few standing bac k to back in the middle of the room. One window on the outside wall allowed for natural lighting, with smaller bookshelves underneath the window sill, with overhead lighting causing shadows along the floor.

"I have more packed up in the basement." I replied as I went over to the fantasy section, "This collection is a combination of my brother's and Elijah's books as well as mine."

Jefferson took one of the books off the shelf, and I held my breath. Jeremy's wife had given him some of those books with loving inscriptions written inside; it might be one of those books.

Jefferson flipped through the book, then back to the beginning.

"ReesesCup, this eliminates your excuses. All my heart, Eli."

I burst out laughing, closing the space to quickly take the book from Jefferson. It was George MacDonald's *The Wise Woman*.[9]

"Can I ask?" Jefferson inquired.

"I love C.S. Lewis," smiling, I flipped through the book, "but I didn't manage to read George MacDonald, whom Lewis admired greatly.

---

[9] MacDonald, George. *The Wise Woman and Other Stories*, 1875.

Elijah praised MacDonald and was shocked that I had never read him. At the time, I was in my sci-fi phase, so I put Elijah off when he suggested I read some of MacDonald's books. Told him, oh, couldn't find him in the library, or I couldn't make it to the bookstore. At the time I was on a kick not to order books online, support your local bookseller, you know. Finally, for my birthday, Elijah presented me with this, as well as a few other books."

"Did you read it" Jefferson asked, "or resist on principle?"

Startled that he knew I had been tempted to do just that, I disguised it by busying myself putting the book back.

"I read it." Walking over to my fantasy section, I retrieved the book. "Here you go."

Jefferson was perusing the shelves, "Do I have to get a library card to borrow from here?"

"No, but I'm going put a note in my calendar that you borrowed this. It's due in 21 days." I replied.

"And if I do not return it on time?"

"Then no more borrowing," I said solemnly. "My library is privately funded, and I must be able to trust its patrons."

Jefferson chuckled, his face lightening. I didn't realized until this moment how sad he had looked.

"You okay?" I asked, before I could think better of it.

His eyes dulled, "Yes. No." With a cynical smile he added, "Why do you ask?"

"You looked sad."

"Since when did you care? You made it clear you do not want to."

The attack wasn't quite vitriolic, more of a lash out tempered by the shadows in his face.

"I would resent that statement," I replied, "if it wasn't true. But," I added in a kinder tone, "it's s not because I'm heartless. For whatever reason you're sad, I'm sorry."

We stared at each other for a moment. He dropped his gaze first, turning to my books.

"What would you give to have your husband back?" His eyes flicked to me briefly before he moved down the row and took down another book.

"Well, the world's not mine to give."

"Nor the stars." Jefferson bent his head down, studying the open book.

> "When you are old and gray and full of sleep,
> And nodding by the fire, take down this book,
> And slowly read, and dream of the soft look
> Your eyes had once, and of their shadows deep.
> How many loved your moments of glad grace,
> And loved your beauty with love false or true,
> But one man loved the pilgrim soul in you,
> And loved the sorrows of your changing face.
> And bending down beside the glowing bars,
> Murmur, a little sadly, how love fled
> And paced upon the mountains overhead,
> And hid his face amid a crowd of stars."[10]

Jefferson, when I first had spoken, had lifted his head, and fixed his eyes on my face.

"W.B. Yeats," I explained, "You are holding a book of his poetry. I won't say he's a favorite poet of mine, but I love that poem. When you said "stars," while holding that book, it made me think of it."

"I can follow that line of thought," Jefferson put the book back. "Shockingly, it fits my mood. They say Yeats wrote that about a woman who rejected him repeatably."

"An actress friend," I supplied.

"She didn't love him like he loved her."

"It's said that Maud Gonne didn't love him at all, not like that." Suddenly, I sensed we were on dangerous ground, but why I couldn't detect. Was it attraction to me or memory of her? "Are we friends, Reisa?" Jefferson asked, breaking into my thoughts.

Drawing a deep breath, I thought about that, "Yes. I believe we are heading there."

"You always do that."

"Do what?"

"I didn't notice it at first, but for a long time you drew a deep breath whenever you saw me. Sometimes you still do, when I have asked about something or someone. Like your brother."

I felt the ice go into my eyes, but I couldn't prevent it. I did not want to talk about Jeremy with Jefferson.

---

[10] Yeats, William Butler. "When You Are Old," 1898.

"See, a reaction. Maybe not a deep breath this time, but that look, you've given it before. You told Ellen I wasn't a good man."

So many ways I could play this. I could point out that I had witnessed him breaking Nicole's heart that day, or I could point out how he aggressive he had been with me. I could claim I was wound up, after the beforementioned fight, and then Nicole going after me.

I do not play games, but it feels like I've played one with him the last year, dancing around my true issue with him.

"You really have somewhere to go?" I asked him.

He narrowed his eyes.

"I want to clear the air, and it will take some time. You said you couldn't stay long," I reminded him, "I can't say everything I need to in a short time." I hugged myself, "Besides, I need some time to think."

"You aren't making any sense. What do you have against me?"

"Please, go; do what you need to do, and then we're talk. Or not. Up to you."

Right now. I will talk to him. It's a matter of when.

Jefferson lowered his brows, inspecting me. "Alright. I have an appointment I'm probably late for. After that, it'll be late, tomorrow? Are you free?"

"Give me a time, and I will be." I'll work tonight to free up tomorrow.

"Eight too early?"

"No. How about we meet at the Overlook? The small clearing near the cliff where you can sit on the rocks and look over the forest."

"I know it," He said, amused.

"Of course, you grew up here." I shook my head, "See? Head not on straight."

I led him to the back door and waited as he put his shoes on.

"Tomorrow, okay?"

"Okay." Whatever ghost that had haunted him when he arrived had been vanquished by confusion. Temporarily at least. With one last quizzical look, Jefferson walked down the deck stairs.

CHAPTER 19

Confessions

At one point, my father, already past middle age, faced a temptation akin to Paul's.

One woman, in her mid-thirties with two elementary-aged children, came to my father, her pastor, for counseling after her divorce. Before, she had attended church service occasionally but, after meeting with Dad, she often popped up, with and without her children, at church events.

Dad was pleased, happy to welcome her in helping the church. At one point, she became active in youth outreach, and my father enjoyed working with the youth. Dad, even past sixty, turned heads with his smile and strong, lanky build. I inherited those eyes, but without that ability to make people glow when I looked at them. The woman—I'm making up a name for her, Molly—obviously developed a crush on Dad, despite the fact that she was an adult with two children. She flirted when she could get away with it, enough though that a sullen, fifteen-year-old caught the flattered expression on Dad's face. As did Mom. Flattered or not, Dad more than loved Mom, he adored her. Anything that may have hurt her he avoided. One youth event, dressed in jeans and a snug shirt, Molly grew bold enough to compliment Dad, noting how he looked quite young and handsome, taking such care with his appearance. This was said not only in front of the youth, but in front of my petite, sixty-year-old Mom, dressed in simple, plain clothing. The contrast between the two was obvious, of course. Mom didn't look young, and she shouldn't have had to worry about trying. I saw that hard look coming to Mom's face, when Dad smoothly and firmly informed Molly that his gorgeous, sweet wife made him feel young. One arm wrapped around Mom, he planted a kiss, tame but sweet, on her lips before leading her away. The only time I saw Mom look smug. Dad must have said something privately to Molly as well, because she avoided Dad after that. Sometimes I caught her glare going Dad's way. I read once that, in the face of temptation, Joseph fled, but David lingered. Just because someone doesn't betray his or her spouse, doesn't mean the chance was not there. No, it's the reaction to that chance. There are those who love their spouses, but hurt them anyway. I won't pretend I understand it, nor can I explain it. I can write self-righteously how I could never do so.

People are weak to certain sins. Some people, who would never steal even an apple, struggle with their temper. Some people gossip, even adding a few tidbits to make it more exciting, but turn their nose up at those fighting alcohol addiction.

Some people battle lust, while never struggling with greed.

So many sins, tailor-fitted to each sinner.

Some people can't forgive and forget. Is that a sin?

—ReesesCup76, The Cost of Forgiving Blog

Early morning texting confirmed Jefferson could still meet with me. I left River behind, not sure how long this would take. I left the letter behind, after thinking about it. Praying over it.

This will be done in steps.

Arriving before Jefferson, I wrapped a shawl around me to protect against the chill before seating myself on a cold rock facing the overlook. Warm light crept like molasses over the trees, highlighting the brown of the unawakened along with the proud colors of the early risers. The sun ascended high in the sky before I heard footsteps coming up the path.

The sound stopped then, in my peripheral vision, I watched Jefferson take a seat on a rock nearby.

I broke the silence.

"My brother died twelve years ago this week."

Jefferson's mouth opened, face apologetic, before his brow furrowed. He spoke in a thoughtful tone,

"Twelve years."

I nodded.

"I'm sorry."

I ignored that.

"My husband died three years ago, after the anniversary of Jeremy's death. We were rock climbing with friends; Elijah wanted to distract me. Details aren't important, nor do I remember exactly what happened that day, no matter how I have tried. Whether it was a rock slide or something else, it ended with Elijah taking the blunt of the rocks, pulling me...." I shook my head, my voice trembling, "I can't remember. I know he saved my life. I know my left leg was pinned under a rock long enough that I almost lost it. I know Elijah's body was so battered there was a closed casket. I was in the hospital; I couldn't even attend his funeral."

> *"I never talk about that time. I spent my time raging at God, but finally, in the quiet of a hospital room, I accepted what I could not understand."*

Jefferson bent over to reach my hand, squeezing it. He released it and sat back.

"I have friends, two in particular who are like sisters, but I lost my family. Lost," I scoffed, "Like I could ever find them again. Not until heaven."

"I've never heard you be bitter before," Jefferson said without rebuff.

I glanced at his face and saw understanding.

"I never talk about that time. I spent my time raging at God, but finally, in the quiet of a hospital room, I accepted what I could not understand." I drew a deep breath which, in turn, drew a smile from Jefferson.

"I'm going to pry, Jefferson. I've been told you were hurt twelve years ago; Ellen shared that with me. I take that with a grain of salt, of course, but...." I had thought long and hard how to approach this subject, but what I had decided on fled my mind. Watching Jefferson, I saw his posture stiffen and a flash of confusion come over his face.

"I wish I could say," I continued, "that whatever happened to you twelve years ago isn't any of my business. It's difficult to explain. Will you tell me your tale? Show me your wounds? If so, I will answer any of your questions. A sad tale in exchange for another sad tale. I'll tell you about Jeremy."

"This is weird," Jefferson commented. "Why would you need to know my story? Are you planning to write about it?"

"No," I instantly denied, turning to him. I refused to make money off this tale. My forgiveness blog hadn't made any money. I didn't tell him that; he didn't need to know of it.

"If you do not share your side," I said, mentally sighing at the slip, "I will still share mine. It works better if we do it this way, but…."

"Fine."

My eyes widened, "Really? So fast? I mean I know I sound crazy."

"You will be shocked at what I've observed about you," Jefferson whispered, "I have felt like a stalker at times. I'm the one who's crazy. If you want my story, okay."

His face turned thoughtful and so sad.

"I loved once, a beautifully fragile woman. She was older than I was and married."

He drew a deep breath, huffing it back out.

"I never thought I would involve myself with a married woman. I believed, still believe, marriage is sacred. When I met her, I fell hard, and starting deluded myself that there are shades of gray. In times when the marriage should end, you are allowed to seek comfort. I was a selfish someone who wanted what he wanted. I met her at a party; the host was her business client and my friend.

"Vivian was…," he swallowed thickly, "She had auburn hair, a soft heart-shaped face, and gentle blue eyes. I noticed her body, of course, but it was her face that drew me in. So sad."

He paused, looking pained.

"People whispered about how Vivi's husband never went anywhere with her anymore. There were hints that they were separated. I befriended her, but I knew I wanted more. I'm not proud of how I slowly seduced her, how I used friendship to win her. I cannot change that. Like you said about choices, I made mine."

His voice stopped, and I stopped rubbing my temple to see him staring at me. My chest hurt, hearing this, but I motioned for him to go on.

"Vivi's husband neglected her. Same old story, right? Husband or wife takes his or her spouse for granted and that spouse stumbles to outside affection. It was worse than that, for her. She took care of everything: running the house, the bills, their side businesses. He didn't work; she supported them both. And he was so needy, not supporting her at these events she had to attend for work, but making her rush home afterwards. Sometimes, when I pressed, Vivi would repeat some of the comments her husband had made. I do not remember them exactly but, at the time, well, they made me angry.

"I pursued her, and she guiltily gave in. I made her happy, I know I did. She smiled more; she appeared lighter. We kept our relationship secret, of course, but my friend, who suspected something, I believe, mentioned to me how different she seemed.

"Then, one day, Vivi told me her husband found out about us. I begged her to leave him, but she refused, saying he needed her." He paled at the memory. "I said things I shouldn't have, accusing her of using me. She had said she loved me, and I had told her I loved her, but I threw that back in her face, saying that she had lied. Twenty-two-year-old males can still be immature." He stopped, his lips thin.

I wanted to say some sarcastic comment, perhaps, but I remained quiet, fighting to keep the emotion off my face.

"No judgment?" he probed.

"Your story over?"

"No."

My mouth twisted, "I'm reserving my sentencing."

"Great, thanks. Well, this part's hard."

Despite knowing the pain coming, I soften a bit, a small voice of compassion whispering in my heart. "As slow as you need."

Encouraged Jefferson sped on.

"I didn't contact her after our fight for a month. Let her miss me, ya know? Childish. Vivi didn't contact me either. Then," his eyes started watering, "I heard her husband had died, I didn't hear how, and that she had killed herself."

He rubbed at his eyes, "No one knew about us, I guess her husband didn't tell anyone. I had to pick up rumors. Some claimed she suffered from depression and her husband's death had broken her."

"How do you not know how her husband died?"

Jefferson's eyes widened then narrowed, and I realized how venomous my words had come out.

"I didn't; it didn't matter."

"Didn't matter?"

"I cared about her, not him," he said bluntly. "And once I knew Vivi's death had been a suicide—they found a note—I didn't stick around. I went to the funeral, but I couldn't stay."

I stared at him, my brow lowered. Judgment fought mercy in my head. He waited, unknowing what I battled with.

Mercy won.

"That makes sense. That fits."

Confused, he opened his mouth, but I held up a hand. Leg aching, I stood up and stretched. Walking a circle around the small area, I came to a stop in front of Jefferson.

"Okay, my turn. Are you up for listening?"

I saw indecision on Jefferson's face. Did he want to say no? Did the indifference turning to anger then indifference again unnerve him? Had I made him furious because I offered no sympathy?

"Go ahead." I return to my seat, a bit farther away so he couldn't touch me.

"I have a brother, as you well know. I guess I should say had a brother, but even though he died, he's forever my brother. He married his high school sweetheart, or really academy sweetheart, since he attended an academy. I didn't know her well, being so much younger than both of them."

I stopped, considering.

"I guess I should add that I was late-life baby. I saw my brother, Jeremy, infrequently as a child. Yet, we were close. I wrote to him, silly little kid things, and he replied to every single one. Whenever he came home, he would take me around with him. Looking back, I realized that wasn't normal, but that was Jeremy. When he loved you, you knew it. Everyone liked him or, I should say, not everyone. Jeremy once told me that everyone wasn't going to like you, some people were going to dislike you no matter how you acted. It's important to accept that and treat them well anyway."

I laughed, surprising myself and Jefferson as well, judging by his startled reaction.

"Sorry, it's just, I sound like a kid. Anyhow, he was far nicer than me. Friendlier as well. I wish I could say I used to be friendly, that his death changed me but, truthfully,—I've attempted to always be truthful to myself—he received the nice genes. His death did change me, how could it not?"

My smile had faded, and I broke eye contact, looking over at the trees. In a measured tone, I spoke again.

"I haven't mentioned my parents. It's sad that they are an afterthought but, by the time I was born, they were old. Jeremy was born when they were already near their forties; my birth came after Mom thought she couldn't conceive any more. Jeremy came by his sweet nature honestly. I always felt loved, if not a bit lonely. Their lives were busy; my father was a pastor and my mother a nurse. Mom had done the whole stay-at-home bit with Jeremy and went back to work when he was school aged."

"You said you were homeschooled." I nodded, my gaze coming back to him, "I was. I spent two or so years at the church school before it closed down. Mom didn't want to send me to public school. It was difficult, but they made schooling me at home work out. Sometimes I went along with…." Heat rushed to my face, mocking the chill of the air.

"Sorry, that's a story, but not the story I want to tell."

Jefferson apologized, "My question led you off topic."

"Nah. Its fine. Just no more questions, I'm easily distracted. Plus, there are areas you may not understand why I would tell you, but it will make sense in the end, okay?"

Jefferson smiled, "Okay."

"Jeremy. He wasn't perfect; it would have been unfair if he had been. We fought; he could be overbearing when he thought he was right. Just so you know I'm not putting him on a pedestal."

This point was important to me, and I waited for some response from him. Jefferson nodded.

"My parents were killed in a car accident when I was in my second year of college. I was in Michigan, and Jeremy flew in from California to tell me because he couldn't bear to share the news over the phone."

My voice thickened, weighted with sorrow, "He took care of everything, made the arrangements for me to go home, took care of their estate, everything—the details aren't important. I went back to school and spent my holidays with Jeremy and his wife. In fact, I ended up transferring to a college in California to be near my only living family. Once I had graduated, I rented an apartment near Jeremy. Close enough to stay in contact, far enough away to give each of us space. We each had our own lives, but Jeremy and I met weekly for lunch, and I was invited to his house ever so often.

"His wife…." I struggled with what to say; he didn't need to know this part.

"I liked her," I finally said. "She was such a delicate little thing, having almost a bird-like quality to her. Fragile, and yet when my parents died, she weathered the storm with Jeremy, supporting him. He adored her. Yes, she had some traits that bothered me, but who am I to judge? I rub most people the wrong way."

I shrugged, unrepentant.

"For a while, I couldn't even identify exactly what bothered me about her. I thought maybe I was jealous of the attention he gave her. That thought I quickly dismissed. I finally decided it was because we were opposite. She seemed to need someone to applaud her, admire her, and entertain her. Some people do. She was so sweet though.

"I worried about Jeremy; he seemed to spend so much time trying to keep her happy. He appeared to succeed; theirs was a happy marriage, and she loved him. When it turned out she couldn't have children, they talked about adoption and decided to wait a few years. She threw herself into work. In fact, her work and work functions came first; he was always skipping his own work events when they coincided with hers. They even relocated when she received a promotion. I didn't follow them; I had an established life at that point. They moved four hours away. Jeremy and I changed our lunches to once a month, on the weekend, meeting halfway. She never came to the lunches, although I told Jeremy she was welcome. I missed her. Jeremy and I only met once a month, but we e-mailed and called frequently, staying close in spirit."

I closed my eyes as I whispered, "Then Jeremy got sick."

Opening my eyes, I focused on the trees below our little platform. There was no disguising the pain in my voice; I felt it radiating, dimming the sun around me.

"He called me up, asking me to meet him. We had already had our monthly meeting, so I knew something was up. I had noticed Jeremy growing thinner, eating less, but he had claimed it was stress. He had had trouble finding a new job when they moved, settling for a contracting job for which work was infrequent. While he enjoyed the work, it could be stressful with deadlines. He admitted he had put off going to the doctor because he was afraid. When he finally did...."

I broke off, remembering that day. It took me several long moments to find my voice again.

"He had pancreatic cancer. They hoped to remove the tumor, but...." I stopped again and rubbed my face. "I can't—the details of what he went through—they aren't important to the story. Just know, it was bad. Very bad."

"Want to stop?" Jefferson asked.

"I can't, not now. This has been years in coming. I helped all I could, but in the end...." All the heat was gone; I felt cold.

"In the end I moved closer to them to help out. His wife would call me, asking me to take him to his treatments or come over to keep him company while she went to some necessary work function. I ended moving into the house.

That's how I noticed that his wife was barely around and, when she was, she was distant. I admit, I got angry. Jeremy had never told me anything about his marriage—he felt strongly about that—but once I was in the house, I saw how much she avoided him. It was such a contrast to before he had gotten sick, when I would visit and she was so affectionate. I researched support groups for spouses of cancer patients, in addition to the materials the doctor had already provided. She wasn't interested in going. Well, she never said that, but whenever there was a meeting she ended up not being able to go. Her work was busy, she told me. She had a lot of stress."

The moment of truth. I prayed silently as I locked my eyes on Jefferson.

"Then, one night, I was picking up some carryout out from Jeremy's favorite restaurant. He had trouble eating, but I hoped....Well, I saw Vivian leaving the restaurant, a man nuzzling her neck as they walked to his car."

Jefferson's eyes widened as comprehension rolled through him. Maybe if I hadn't suggested I had issues with him, he wouldn't have been so quick to notice her name. I saw his face pale. My own stomach turned, in memory. How strong betrayal was to revolt even the bit players.

My mouth kept moving as I thought, telling the tale I longed not to relive.

"Confronting her when she got home, she pleaded with me not to tell Jeremy. That she would end it. She had needed someone; it was hard seeing her husband die. I've never hated anyone like I hated her."

"Did, did you tell..." He started asking, his voice hoarse, before I cut him off.

"I didn't have to make that difficult decision. He heard us fighting. It gave me sick pleasure to watch her crumble, or it would have if it haven't been for Jeremy. Some people get angry when faced with a death sentence, some make peace, some grow closer to God. Jeremy displayed in his final days, an amount of empathy and understanding I didn't think even he was capable of."

Shock wove through my senses, despite the years between then and now, years of accepting.

"He forgave her. This broken mess of a woman on the floor, where she had dramatically thrown himself at his feet. Like the prophet Hosea in the Bible, who kept taking his wayward wife back, Jeremy knelt before his wife and granted mercy. She didn't deserve it. She broke the marriage vows in her weakness, but judging her—you never know what breaks a person." I drew a deep breath, "You know she ended the affair. Vivian threw herself into caring for him. She admitted to me she had never told anyone at work that he was sick. Only her non-work friends knew, and you wouldn't have known them." It was too late; Jeremy died less than two weeks after I confronted Vivian. He thanked me." Shocked still, after all these years, I repeated, "He thanked me for holding back my personal opinions on his marriage. He knew how I felt about her, and he asked me to forgive her. I told him she doesn't need my forgiveness; she didn't sin against me. Jeremy told me I needed the forgiveness, or I would become bitter."

Some people get angry when faced with a death sentence, some make peace, some grow closer to God. Jeremy displayed in his final days, an amount of empathy and understanding I didn't think even he was capable of.

I looked at Jefferson, not fighting the emotions now. Traces of loathing choked me; I thought I conquered them.

"You know Vivian killed herself. After the funeral, I told her about Jeremy's last request of me. I said I forgave her, despite the sin not being against me. Basically, I lied, even though I can claim I tried. She didn't know what to say. Her suicide note was addressed to me; she wanted me to know that she appreciated my forgiveness, but that she disagreed with me about my forgiveness being necessary. She needed it, but she couldn't forgive herself." I stopped. "This will be painful for you to hear, given that you still love her. She wrote that Jeremy was her world; and she was lost when he got sick."

Jefferson's eyes turned wretched. Despite knowing now what lies Vivian had told, love still survived. Jealousy as well—stronger than death, it appears.

"But she loved you also."

I did not want to be cruel, even if this was ripping me apart. Jefferson's mouth dropped slightly.

"She didn't understand how she could love two men, but she did. Her love for you was new and exciting, but still love. The reason she didn't return to you? Losing Jeremy, she lost someone who knew her faults. She had built her relationship with you on lies. She knew you, but you didn't really know her. She felt that, when you found out all the lies she had told you, you would be as disgusted with her as I was."

"She told you my name. You didn't seek me out to tell me?" Jefferson flared, misplaced anger in his eyes. I scowled at him.

"She never asked me to. She gave me your name, yes, but I owed you nothing. I do not know even why she gave me your name, only your first name. To find you, I would have had to reveal why I needed to find you. Her affair would have been revealed, and I know Jeremy wouldn't have wanted that. He wouldn't have want her memory tainted."

"Yet, you found me."

"I didn't know you lived here until I had already moved. I recognized you from that night, from the funeral—yes, I saw you—and from the photos she left me."

How bitter I had felt that day I found those photos.

"I wasn't about to give up the peace I had found here, so I avoided you." I reminded him, "I saw you that night; I saw how you were with her...." I broke off, getting up off the rock. Reaching into my pocket I pulled out a necklace. Vivian's necklace, the locket Jefferson had given her.

"Jeremy's will divided his assets between her and me. Vivian had made a new will right after Jeremy died. She left everything to me. Her parents and sister weren't pleased," I gave a flat smile. "I didn't want her money or things. I picked out the family heirlooms Jeremy had given her, and I found this. Since I knew your name, I figured that these were your initials."

He reached out his hand, and I dropped the necklace into his hand, carefully. He pulled his hand back, caressing the initials on the heart with his thumb: "To V.L with love J.H."

"I gave the rest of her things to her parents and sister. It's what they wanted anyway, mementos of her. If you have anything else you want back, ask them."

He stared at the locket, "You still hate her."

And like that, anger deflated, leaving pain.

"It's funny, for the first eleven years I kept that hate frozen, not letting the fire of forgiveness near it. I've learned a lot about forgiveness this past year. For some, they make that decision, and it's done. For others, it's a daily occurrence, a choice you make each day consciously until one day you realize you do not have to think about it anymore. You are free. I'm working on that, I'm hoping that this—I hoped this would heal that part of me, and perhaps you as well. After what I couldn't help overhearing Nicole say to you…." I caught myself. "I didn't want to know you still suffered. I knew you must have loved her, I saw you at the funeral with your heart bleeding, and I wanted you to hurt. Jeremy hurt, too."

Lump in my throat, I bowed my head.

"I made a mistake. I tried to forgive her, but I transferred the rage I felt to you instead. I struggled with it. You knew she was married; she told me that," my smile disappeared. "It was a very informative letter she left me, more like a confession. To the only remaining living person who knew the depth of her betrayal."

Jefferson looked devastated. I became aware of water dropping from the trees, and I pulled the hood of my jacket up. Hugging myself, I waited, my part done.

I wanted this finished.

"Everything I thought I knew about Vivian, about our affair," Jefferson mused. "How black, how cruel. I remembered that night, being so happy. It was the next day that Vivian met me for lunch, breaking off our affair. She looked like she haven't slept. She lied then too, about why." Jefferson stopped, looking lost in thought.

"Lies, the pillars of adultery, built on lust. Sorry, not lust, but love, you claim. That was mean. Sorry."

The wound flared to life, the emotional toil greater than even the physical pain I suffered. On my feet the moment of my last "sorry," I walked away.

After a few yards, Jefferson caught up with me. Darting in front of me, hair damp from the light rain, he stopped me.

"Where are you going?" he demanded.

"Home. Look, we can avoid each other, now that you know."

"You hate me."

"Um, yes, sometimes," I said, surprised at the discovery. My words rushed out unchecked, barely thought, "My brother's heart broke, and though Vivian was the one who broke the vows, you admittedly weren't innocent. Your choice to pursue her led to her having a choice. Her choice to have an affair led to me moving in, since her time became consumed with you. I had more time with my brother, but my choice to move in led me to witnessing you two together, and so forth. If you could undo your action...."

I paused, then continued.

"Yeah, I would have my brother's heart not be broken, because forgiving or not, it sped up his dying. He was devastated, but his love for her was greater than that hurt. He understood, in a way I never could."

I saw the tears building in his eyes.

"I'm sorry," he choked, "I was a stupid, selfish kid."

"You loved her."

"Yes," he admitted.

"You still love her."

"God help me, yes. She lied, yes, but I know I knew her, despite the lies."

"Go on thinking that." My lip curled before I caught myself. "Sorry, sorry. I cannot tell you how you feel. I cannot do this any longer. I thought you would...."

"Would hate her?"

Why do we have to do this part? I shook my head.

"I assumed you would get away from me as soon as you could. Hold on to your memories, ignore the truth. The Vivian you knew wasn't the one I did, beyond surface similarities. She was delicate, sweet, and so very, very weak in many ways. Maybe I demonized her by how she was at the end. I'm tired of her ghost hanging around you. I see you and I see her. You may have moved away to get away from her memory, but memories do not work like that. They follow you. She wasn't a fragile woman you tried to save, she was a weak woman who used you."

Jefferson's breathing turned labored, his jaw clutched.

I nodded at what I saw in his eyes, confirmation of my beliefs. I stepped around him, and he didn't stop my leaving.

CHAPTER 20

The Letter

That's my side of what happened. I won't give names or tell his side. Not in unfairness, but I do not feel I have the right to.

Remember, there are two sides to a coin.

Not that affairs should be justify.

I went to meetings, hoping to find others struggling as I was. I sat and listened to others' stories, stories that inspire dramas and women's fiction. One woman related how her husband's mistress turned up at his funeral. The wife had no idea of the mistress's existence, whereas the mistress had been fully aware of the wife's. Another woman told about how she had no idea her husband had had a child from the affair he admitted to years ago. She found out when the mother of the child died, and the child came to live with her biological father, the husband. Of course, wives betray also. Men told of their wives sleeping with their friends, their brothers, even their sisters. I stopped attending the recovering from adultery and guilt meetings before my own turn came around. What can I say? I had two stories I could tell, and one didn't involve me directly, rather it was a betrayal of one I loved. I wondered aloud how these people at the meetings could forgive, and not one could answer that question. They struggled, clinging to each other in comfort, yet alone. They had to forgive on their own. Pastors overseeing their meetings would quote texts of comfort, encouraging them to forgive, as God forgives. I acknowledged that, but I still found myself hurting time and again. Problem is the hurt comes because I cannot resolve my hate. I cannot confront the one who wounded the one I loved. She's beyond that.

I attended these meetings for another reason as well. I had been engaged when I left to care for my brother. My time with Jeremy left my fiancé at loose ends. Sometime after the events around Jeremy's death had played out and I was trying to settle back into my life, I became instantly aware of what distance can do. I saw my fiancé coming out of a cafe shop, thirty minutes after canceling on me for lunch. The woman he was with was sweet. Like I said earlier, sweet people can still hurt you. There was a flash of guilt and understanding in her eyes as I stood there stunned. We had met before, and she had been nice. Ethan—yes, his real name—stumbled for words to explain away why he was, moments before, holding this woman's hand and leaning into her. Why he was lifting his free hand to her face. I'm not emotionless. Sarcastic, yes. Abrupt at times, yep. But I hurt, and I cry. Tears welled up in my eyes that day. In less than a month, I had lost those I trusted most. Two broke that trust, one died. I left them standing there—wondering if I was overreacting—but memories of broken dates, of the increasingly distant way he acted toward me, told another story. He came over that night, knocking then pounding on my door. I know this because a neighbor informed me. I wasn't home. I went to Selene's. I ignored his phone calls, texts, and e-mails for five days, before a friend convinced me I should face him and move on. We met in the cafe, neutral territory. In that long conversation, I discovered how much he resented my close relationship with my brother. I received closure in that I could confront him but, at that meeting, my heart shut off.

It took five years, and a rather determined man, to turn it back on. Oh, I dated before I met my husband, but I didn't trust. The romance with my husband, for it was a romance…what can I say? Eros love cannot save your soul but, my husband, he helped in healing my relationship with God.

I've never, even after my husband died, lost that bond.

A story for another time, if you want to read it of course.
Going back to forgiveness. Has talking to the other man, so to speak, helped me in my path to forgiveness?
I wonder, if instead, I didn't drag someone else to hell.
—ReesesCup76, The Cost of Forgiving Blog

The early morning sun snuck past the gap in the curtains, mocking the dimness of the bedroom light with its superior illumination. I turned away, onto my right side, phone in the other hand as I spoke.

"Much of life is waiting for other's reactions, no matter what you say or do, no matter if you pick and poke, other people are in control once the words are out there."

Selene sighed, the sound coming loud and clear through the phone. I snuggled deeper into the warmth of my bed, keeping my mouth clumped shut before I echoed her sigh.

"I don't know if I agree with you Rei, some people excel at producing the reactions they desire. Still, in this case, yeah, it's out of your control."

"It's been five days."

"And how many years have you had this knowledge? Give the guy a break."

My turn to sigh.

"Maybe I was wrong to dump this on him."

"Confronting him you mean. If he had stayed a stranger, if he had left you alone, perhaps. Doesn't he deserve to know the results of his actions?"

"Do we always know the depths of pain our sins cause in others? Should we? The burden of what we've done—if we knew everything, none of us could stand. In unburdening myself, did I just dump that burden on another?"

"Were your shoulders intended to carry the burden? No Reisa, you need to heal, and with him hanging around you, this had to be laid in the open."

"This wound has bled freely for far too long."

"Exactly."

"Thanks, Selene."

We said our good-byes, and I pushed "End," still not convinced. Has anything really changed? Years of not saying Vivian's name, years of keeping her photos locked away, even the ones with Jeremy, has that anger really vanished?

The human mind can torment one into action, then torture one about whether the action was necessary afterwards. Did I pray enough, did I think this over?

It is what it is, can't undo it.

With that truth, I curled up in my bed again. River at my feet, Sebastian by my head, on the pillow he claimed as his, I stared at my wedding photo on the wall.

I miss Eli so much, his advice, his support, whether we agreed or not, he helped me clear my thoughts. Can I fool myself really though; I miss everything, his smell, his laugh, his arms around me.

> *Forty years old within touch, a widow, a cripple, turning into a crazy pet lady. I started laughing, causing two animals to peer at me in alarm.*

Forty years old within touch, a widow, a cripple, turning into a crazy pet lady. I started laughing, causing two animals to peer at me in alarm.

"I'm feeling sorry for myself," I explained to them, which made me laugh all the harder. "Oh. This is ridiculous!"

I threw the covers back, dislodging my dog, who fled the bed for her own, and the cat disappeared out the door as well. After taking a nice long, hot shower, I dressed in jeans and a sweatshirt. Comfy socks pulled over my feet, I padded down the hallway to my office. Work, the cure for ignoring reality.

A loud knocking, or rather banging, coming from the front door, awaken my senses to the dying light pouring from the window. I grabbed the plate with its remains of my lunch and exited the office.

Dropping the plate off in the kitchen sink, I hobbled down the stairs to the front door, my footfalls matching the repetitive knocking on the door.

Peeking through the side window revealed Jefferson. He looked over at the window, his hand dropping to his side.

I pulled back, unlocking the front door and opening it, about to make a comment on impatience when he cut my words off.

"I want to see the letter." He crossed his arms, his face taut.

I waved him inside and shut the door after him. Standing in the small foyer, I met his eyes, noticing the stubborn clenching of his jaw.

"Not sure if that's a great idea. But…" I added before he could voice protest, "why not."

Lip tingling from my sharp teeth as I bit back any more words, I walked up the stairs, Jefferson following behind. Walking over to the end table, near the front window, I picked up the envelope. Pausing a moment, I threw a glance over my shoulder at Jefferson.

He came over to stand next to me.

"That's it?"

I turned my gaze downward, to the writing on the envelope, rubbing my thumb over it. Kinda obvious it was.

"You were expecting me?" he asked, as he extended his hand for the letter I held.

"I wasn't sure. No, it's out because I read it again last night. Are you up for this?"

"Please." He kept his hand out.

"It doesn't leave the house; you will have to read it here."

Surprised marked both our faces at my outburst. Until that moment, I had never considered how I felt about letting the letter leave my possession. I'll analyze why later. I waited for his acknowledgment.

"Okay," he finally said.

I handed the letter to him and motioned to the couch. He walked over and sank down. Opening the envelope, he pulled out the letter and unfolded the pages.

I handed the letter to him and motioned to the couch. He walked over and sank down. Opening the envelope, he pulled out the letter and unfolded the pages.

"I don't hate you," I mumbled, and he glanced quizzically up. "What I said earlier, the pain was fresh."

He lowered the pages, his face a question. I sat down in the chair near the couch.

"Before you read that, I just wanted you to know that. It's funny, for my brother's sake, I want to still hate you but, at the same time, he would want me not to. I thought about this, the last few days, trying to figure out my emotions so I do not have to think about it again. If I had met you then, I think I could have hated you, the man you were then. The man you admitted you were. I met you afterward, this man you've become...."

I glanced down, "I do not know who you were then, and I'm not sure of you now. Yeah, just wanted to say that."

"I was naive," Jefferson admitted, his face softening, "I refused to see anything but what I wanted to see. I read over some of my old journals," he smile slightly, "the ones Vivi teased me about keeping. I think I knew then that she lied about her husband, I just wanted her so much I wanted to believe she didn't love him. That he didn't love her. But he did, didn't he?"

"Very much," I said, my voice low.

"Let me read this; I need to."

I blew out a slow breath, why delay any longer?

"Would you like something to drink?"

"Yes, please. Thank you."

I got up and went into kitchen, the words on the pages following behind me like a ghost. I had read that letter so many times, I knew it by heart.

>Dearest ReesesCup,
>
>You probably don't want me to call you that. How you must hate me! Oh, sweetheart, you are dear to me, you always were. How could I not love you when Jeremy loved you so very much.
>
>Okay, I'll admit at times I was jealous of how close you two were, but that jealousy could never last. Jeremy was always clear about how much he loved me, and you made so little demands on his time. You always included me when you invited him somewhere. Even to those lunches. Even when I could tell you wanted private time with your brother. I saw that, and that's why I never attended those lunches, not because I didn't love you, but because you willingly shared your brother with me, and I wanted to return the favor.
>
>In case you ever wondered.
>
>I'm trying to think of what you may think, what you may feel, and I apologize for rambling on.
>
>I have no excuse for what I have done. I have spoiled the little time Jeremy had left, and who knows how much longer he might have lived if I hadn't broken his heart. That sin has become too great for me to bear. I wish I had Jeremy's faith,

believing no sin too great for forgiveness. I betrayed my dying husband, physically and emotionally. How can that be forgiven?

Meeting Jefferson…I struggle with regretting that. Another reason to hate me. I've been so selfish, with both Jeremy and Jefferson. Jeremy made me his world's center and, when he got sick, I felt abandoned. How horrible is that! My husband was concentrating on surviving and I was whining he didn't pay enough attention to me!

Watching my handsome Jeremy fade away, I died a bit each day. I would go to work, and there I could pretend everything was like it was before. That's why I told no one at work. My work life and my personal life were so separate; it was rare for the two to intersect. No one knew about Jeremy's illness, and so I didn't have to figure out how to handle all the personal questions that would be asked. I know the rumors that went around when Jeremy could no longer attend events with me. In order to stop that, I would have had to explain why. I was going to, I really was.

Then I meet Jefferson.

He was young, Reisa, much younger than I, younger than you. For some reason, he zeroed in on me, and I couldn't help but be flattered. He offered friendship, easy banter, and later, love.

I fell in love with him, Reisa.

But I still loved Jeremy.

I cannot write *loved*, because I love Jeremy even now that he's gone. I won't give details of my affair with Jefferson. You do not want to know them, and you hate me enough already. I know you offered forgiveness. That you sought me out and offered that to me, well, it shows how tender your heart really is. You would disagree, I know.

Jeremy marveled to me once how you never seemed to notice how loving you really were. Yes, you could be sarcastic and sometimes too much of a loner, but people liked you anyway. You have a goodness in you. You never would have been as weak as I was. I do not write this to flatter you. I resent, on some level, knowing how much stronger you are than me. When you confronted me about the affair, I was on the edge of leaving Jeremy for Jefferson. I wanted to be happy. Then that collapse under the weight of reality. As much as I loved Jefferson, I could not leave Jeremy. Jefferson loved the person I lied about being, Jeremy knew who I am and loved the real me. Even now, thinking about how Jeremy reacted when he overheard us, how understanding he was….I deserve hell for betraying such a man.

You could never hate me as much as I hate myself.

Jefferson will always have my love, and I hurt him deeply. If he knew my lies, it would hurt him even more. I will leave it up to you to decide whether he will ever know.

I've changed my will, leaving everything I have and Jeremy gave me to you. Do with my things what you wish. I'm taking my life, knowing it's not my own to take, because the pain….I know if I continue to live, I will find Jefferson or he will find me, and I won't be able to resist him. I do not want to have a happy ending. I do not deserve it.

I love you Reisa, like a sister. If my death hurts you, I am sorry for that. It's selfish, but I hope you have some love still for me.

Love,

Vivi

P.S. If you ever encounter Jefferson, and that's a big "if," let him know how very sorry I was for my selfishness. He was innocent. He knew I was married, yes, but he thought Jeremy was a horrible husband. I didn't correct his assumptions. To my shame, I even repeated things that I said to Jeremy in my anger, but attributing the words to Jeremy. Jeremy was never cruel to me.

I placed the drink on the side table next to the couch and sat down in the chair again. Waiting, always waiting.

Jefferson looked up after a few moments, heartsickness in those eyes. I glanced down, unable to look at the pain.

Out of the corner of my eye, I saw him fold up the letter and replace it in the envelope.

"Finished?" I stood up and took the letter.

"She wasn't who I thought she was. That letter, that barely sounded like her." He stood.

"And now you have to mourn another death, the death of your idealized Vivian," I said.

"You wanted to spare me that."

I went to the window, standing with the sun at my back to look at him. Hugging myself, I answered. "Yes, but not enough to hold back the existence of the letter. I should have kept my mouth shut."

"No undoing the past," Jefferson said, then wincing, "Sorry."

"No, you are right. Even if the past was only this last week."

"The way you talked about her, Vivian, well, did you love her? I thought you two liked each other at one point but, in that letter, she said she considered you a sister."

"Wow, you do like to draw blood, don't you?" I replied, with no bite, only pain. "I've had years to bury that love."

I thought over the past, how I had fallen apart after my parents' death. Jeremy and I healed together, Vivian sustained us. She gave us a sounding board when we didn't want to burden each other. Vivian checked up on me when I went back to college, sending me care packages like my mother used to. It was she who had suggested I transfer closer to Jeremy.

With a strangled breath I mused aloud, "Do you know I haven't said her name in years? As if that could lessen the hurt. Pain unnamed still aches. Why am I telling you this?" Chest aching, I sat on the chair. River trotted to me. Faithful. Of course, she only showed up now, with all the noise one would think she'd at least bark.

Feeling cold, I slipped to the floor, my arms around my dog. "We had our issues, but with sisters you do not always have to be compatible. Yes, at one point, I thought of her as my sister. My weak, loving, sweet sister." I looked over to the letter, "I guess I still do, deep down."

A wan face, pale with exhaustion, observed my actions, whispering, "That's why you needed to forgive her because, on some level, she betrayed you, too."

"It's more than that. Maybe that as well. It's logical to feel certain emotions, yet emotions can defy logic. Feeling betrayed isn't logical."

"You aren't logical," Jefferson commented, "You strive to appear so, but you aren't."

"How do you know? Really?"

"Something my brother said to me the other day." Changing the subject Jefferson asked, "Did she have any photos, of us? I thought she did...." His voice drifted off briefly, "I thought that's what her husband...."

"Jeremy."

"What Jeremy found."

Grabbing the arm of the chair, I struggled to my feet. River whined. Giving her a reassuring pat, I told Jefferson to follow me.

Down the stairs, through the foyer, down another set of stairs going to the basement. There was a bathroom off the little hallway, where I kept the litter box. Jefferson peeked in the bathroom as we passed. Sebastian gave us an insulted look from his litter box.

"Oops, sorry." Jefferson said, amused.

The second door led to the garage, the door at the end of the left led to the basement. I entered, flicking on the lights.

"Wow, this is even more impressive than your library."

Rows of shelves lined three of the four walls, with two rows, double sided, in the middle of the room. Rubbermaid containers and boxes filled most of the shelves, carefully labeled and sorted. Some shelves contained various items such as lamps.

"I inherited everything," I explained, "After Jeremy's death, all my parents' possessions came to me, as well as Jeremy's. Mom was an only child, so I have the things passed down from her parents, plus Dad's things, as well as Elijah's. This isn't all. Some of the larger things are in storage, or I've lent them out to friends. Stay here, please."

I disappeared among shelves. Vivian's possessions, the few I had kept, were in storage well in the back.

Jefferson didn't listen, coming up behind me as I pulled down a tub. Ignoring him, I removed the lid, taking a small photo box out. My limbs felt a bit heavy as I stood up, opening the box.

Removing a pile of photos, bound with a rubber band, I handed it to him.

"This bunch."

I shut the small box up, concealing the photos of Vivian with Jeremy. Jefferson saw them anyway, his jaw clenching. Jealousy? Really? It wasn't his feelings that I was trying to spare. It just felt wrong to share those photos with him.

"Take these," I indicated the pile he held, "I do not want them."

"I'm not sure I do."

"Then burn them." Replacing the box into the container, I started to lift the container but Jefferson, stuffing the photos in his pocket first, grabbed it and placed it on the shelf. I thanked him.

"Just when I think you are beyond anger, you let loose with a comment like that."

I met his eyes squarely, "I have only one photo of her hanging up, and you can't tell it is her. Should it really surprise you I wouldn't want photos of you two together?"

"No," his voice gentled, "It doesn't."

Leaving the room, I waited for Jefferson to pass me before I shut the door.

"Living here, with the remainders of ghosts, don't you get lonely?"

My lip quirked, "That sounds almost poetic."

Jefferson search my face, as I lifted my brows in question.

"The heart of the house," he said, "did your brother really use that phrase or was it Vivian?"

"It's not unique, really. Jeremy, he had heard something similar as a kid. He liked it enough to use it. Jeremy was a poet, a published poet, in fact. Not that publishing makes your work better but, well, he loved words. The crafting of words to create an image, how a phrase can invoke an emotion."

What the heck. I'm spilling information left and right. Time for him to go.

Jefferson climbed the stairs. His boots still on, I just noticed that, he headed for the door. As the door opened, he paused.

"Twelve years, nearly, and I dated the first few. I gave up because I couldn't find someone I loved, that measured up. That wasn't fair to the women that I dated so as not to feel alone—not because I actually cared about them. I'm not afraid to be alone, and I stopped trying. When I moved here, some understood, some didn't. That didn't matter to me. It's selfish to take when you cannot give, and I had been selfish long enough."

Jefferson turned thoughtful for a moment, "A year ago, I met a woman who interested me. From the first, which surprised me. She was pretty, but not more than other women I knew. Plus, she was more of a loner than I. After fighting it for months, I found out who she was from Ellen," he supplied with a self-deprecating twist of his mouth, "And I found out all I could about her. Not much, outside of business things."

He dropped the facade, "I saw nothing about your brother or your accident. Nothing in your blog, in the forewords to your stories, to prepare me for what you told me."

He scoffed, "I'm not a humble man, but this, this, has humbled me. To find out...." he shook his head, "Yeah, I'm a Christian man, yet it took finding out that Vivian and I had an affair while her husband, your brother, was dying, makes me repent. Marriage is sacred, unless I decide it's not. Anyway, that's off subject. I met you, and I discovered I had a heart still."

I felt heavy, so heavy, in heart and mind. "Jefferson."

"What did you expect telling me would do?" he asked.

Ah, the true question.

"I wanted to forgive," I replied honestly, compelling me to add, "and forget."

"Forget what happened?"

"Forget the pain." I shivered, the spring breeze chilling me. "Or I wanted to think so.

Vivian's actions, she hurt Jeremy. He was devastated, but he must have found peace in forgiving." I want to offer an opinion, but that betrayal was between them.

"She used me," I told Jefferson, "I loved my brother, and she used that. Getting out of things, of appointments where she should have supported him, she disappeared."

"You resented that."

"I know what love is," I replied, "I've seen selfishness as well. Cancer can change a people, both the one with cancer and those around them. I could understand not wanting to see him die.... No, I did see him die, each day, and I counted each moment painfully precious. Even his death, because then he had no more pain. She missed so much with him. She chose to give it up, yet claimed to love him."

"You gave up your life to take care of him."

I wrapped my arms my chest, "Oh, yes. I gave up my cozy life."

Jefferson stared at me, thrown off by the bitterness.

"It cost me, yes, that time away from my normal life.," I shook my head, "No, I did not stop living to care for him. Life is lived no matter where you are, what one means is that you stop doing what you wanted to do."

Borderline pushing him out the door, I said, "Make sense of that."

Determination lit his face, "I will."

I didn't mean it as a challenge.

CHAPTER 21

Ethan

Someone said to me that I gave up my life to care for my brother.

Yep. Gave up a fiancé who apparently got tired of waiting for me to come back. He got tired of canceled dates, and planning to visit and my having to cancel because my brother had an appointment or something and his wife had disappeared.

I can understand why my fiancé, in retrospect, cheated. A breakdown in communications.—No, I <u>can</u> blame him for cheating instead of breaking up with me.

Everyone had a choice, a God-given right, and their choices affected other people, who then chose how to respond. I lost my job, my fiancé, and my lifeline.

My sister-in-law used me, and I resented that I could never work through it with her. I resented that she deprived me of herself. She made a choice that one cannot come back from. Not in this life.

And is that the heart of matter? I'm not sure. These emotions are complicated, aren't they? A knot that won't be untangled, pulled so tightly that one cannot see the separate ropes.

Confronting doesn't work, for me at least. If I exorcised the demon, so to speak, shouldn't it flee? The ghost of her betrayal

> reopened that period in my life. I hadn't thought about it, the details and events, but now they flowed like a river with the dam removed. More later.
>
> —ReesesCup76, The Cost of Forgiving Blog

I blinked then bed my eyes, dry from staring at the computer screen. Won't my brain shut up with the memories? What have I started by this quest? Demons of pain popping up.

Ethan, that jerk. Funny, I remembered the smell of the cafe where we met better than the sound of his voice as he spewed out his resentment over my relationship with Jeremy.

"He needed me." Weary as memories flashed through my head, I broke eye contact and looked out the window. The day promised rain, but the sun still shone.

"This sounds bad but, honestly, his wife should have been by his side. You being there made it so he couldn't have time with Vivian."

Chest tightening, I stared at him.

Ethan's lip firmed into a line, "Vivian told me, we talked, once. She mentioned how you took care of everything. She sounded, bitter."

"Bitter or relieved?"

"She knew you two were close, and...," Ethan's eyes widened as he met my gaze, "I'm sorry, I'm sorry, this is wrong. I know it's too late."

Is this a heart attack? Heart's not stopping, in fact, it's racing.

"You are right, it's too late. I took care of everything because Vivian was gone," my lips twisted. "She was busy with someone else."

"What?" Ethan looked confused.

"Vivian was having an affair." I told him about the weeks before that, how I came to the restaurant in hopes Jeremy would eat his favorite food. "That's when I saw Vivian coming out of a restaurant with her lover, two weeks before Jeremy died."

Ethan's mouth dropped.

"Jeremy knew; I wasn't quiet when I confronted her at home. He forgave her." My chest started hurting. "I shouldn't have told you; he wouldn't want anyone to know."

I bent down, grabbing my bag off the floor. Withdrawing my wallet from the bag, I pulled some money out. Tossing it on the table, I returned my wallet to the bag and stood. Ethan was frozen, his eyes following my motions, but appearing unable to speak.

"I'm not my brother. I cannot understand how, when I needed you most, you could cheat on me. I called you the day Jeremy died, at the office, where I was told you left early, then on your cell, and finally at your house. You were with her, weren't you?"

Ethan unfroze, running a hand over his face, "I regret that. I had no idea."

"You would have if you had been answering my e-mails, my calls, and if you had come to see me as we arranged. I will not regret being there for my brother. He was dying, not peacefully, but painfully. His wife was hiding from that, from everything. I needed you," my voice broke.

Ethan jumped up, reaching for me. I allowed myself one second in his arms, one second of comfort, before remembering why we were here. Pulling back, I wiped at my eyes, acknowledging then ignoring the curious glances we received from other patrons. They probably thought we were breaking up. Well, we were. I pulled off his ring, put it back in its box, out of my bag, holding it out to him.

"No, Reisa." He lifted both hands up. "Please."

How could he appear so surprised and horrified? He must have known this would happen. I placed the box on the table, my movements slow. I felt the guilt, the toll of overwrought emotions, I wanted far away from this pain. This man. One final blow, it appeared, to the Reisa that was. That Reisa thought herself wise, able to cope with pain. I moved around Ethan, but he moved with me. That's right, he never cared about PDA (public displays of affection) or fighting in public. Notice how he had had no problem being affectionate with her in public. She has a name, I remember it now. Ann.

"Go, be with Ann. Give her the ring. I pray she never goes through what I have, and discovers…"

I bit off my words, unnecessarily cruel. I can't be cruel, I'm too tired.

"I wouldn't curse everyone with this," I said with a sigh. I looked at him, than glanced away. A woman gave me a sympathetic smile. She was close enough to hear us without trying to. I nodded slightly, wanting to acknowledge compassion in this horrible moment. I pushed past Ethan, leaving the cafe. He appeared moments later, running to catch up with me.

"I made a mistake," Ethan said, pulling on me to stop. I didn't want to look at him anymore. "I've been so selfish. I was looking at everything wrong. I got everything wrong."

"What clued you in?"

I grimaced as I move out of the line of traffic on the sidewalk, hovering near the building wall. Ethan moved in front of me. "This last five days, I have been thinking so much on how I've acted. Still, I came here ready to justify it. It felt so good to have someone pay attention to me." He stopped at the look I gave him.

"That's what she said—,you know, Vivian," I informed him.

Ethan closed his eyes briefly, then opened them, his gaze sharper, "I'm not her. We aren't married. I made a mistake, a mistake that hurt two people. Ann, she was trying to help, I do not know how to explain how we crossed the line."

"I don't need to hear this!" I shook my head, "It's still about you, about your needs. I can't forgive you, I'm too spent."

Ethan's face turned gray, "I love you."

"Do you? Is this what love does when faced with a crisis? Hide in another person's arms? I can't do this; everything's a mess, I have to put my life together. Without you."

He fought the breakup, like he should have fought temptation. I loved him once, didn't I? Why couldn't I forgive him?

Closing my laptop I moved to the deck. Sitting down, I gazed over the forest. The weather was warmer, the flowers I planted around the garden livening up the green grass. If I planted some more flowers, away from the house, could I see them from the office window?

I wonder where Ethan is now.

"Oh man," I rubbed at one eye, chuckling. "My mind is all over the place."

River stood up, wagging her tail. Her silky fur felt warm under my hand, "Aren't you becoming a sun worshiper," teasing, I added, "Next thing you know, Sebastian and you will fight over the sunbeams coming through the window. I would let the cat win; his claws are sharp."

River closed her eyes, soaking up the petting. I closed my eyes as well. Years upon years of repressed memories flowed through the TV of my mind. Vivian, laughing, as she helped me into my first strapless dress. She took me to my first cocktail party that night, at one of her client's houses. Jeremy, a big grin on his face, escorted us. Vivian, at the lake, dancing under the stars with Jeremy as I snapped their photo.

Ethan, on our first date, taking me to a carnival—somewhere I'd never gone. He kissed me that night, a perfect romantic kiss, as we waited in line at the spin-a-whirl. Ethan again, a bashful look on his face, as he kneeled on the beach, ring in hand. He told me later, upon discovering from Jeremy that our church didn't approve of jewelry, he had almost brought a watch instead. I loved the simple ring, with a small ruby instead of a diamond.

Jeremy, cheesily mugging for the camera I pointed at him during our first "photo shoot." His patient instructions in the darkroom, guiding me through the steps.

The nights my child-self curled up at Jeremy's side and made up tales. The day, years later, when I presented him with my first published story. The times when I started crying, having remembered something Dad said, or something Mom did, and Jeremy would wrap me in his arms.

Elijah, in some ways, reminded me of my brother.

Oh, Elijah. I brushed impatiently at the tears welling up. Pain upon pain hit me, as flashes of memory of that day shot my heart. Elijah, grabbing me, shielding me with his body as the rocks came down, unable to move me because of my pinned leg. I should have been crushed under his weight as well as the rocks. I said I didn't remember much from that day, but I remember Elijah desperately trying to free me. I screamed at him to leave, him roaring he would rather die with me.

I didn't want to live without him. It took a year, more really, for me to accept God's hand in letting me live when I should have died.

Tears escaped my closed lids. Elijah, with his gruff face and mellow voice. I, who always loved a person's eyes, had fallen in love with Eli's voice. Another may not have found it remarkable; I could have spent years listening to him.

I loved Ethan, once, but it was sweet and tame. A whisper, and it could float away. Isn't betrayal more like a shout? That wiped most of the memory of my love as well.

Elijah, there was passion, of course, but more than that, it was a steadying love. He loved me through our fights; he loved me through my random moments of insanity. Two introverts found each other, he said, and to their shock found the one person whose presence renewed their spirit.

I don't live for Elijah; I live because I have no choice. My life is not my own, as tempted as I was to take it; my life came at a cost. A cost I cannot pay. This world dims in light of the next, but I will dwell in it to have the hope of seeing everyone I've lost.

As if I went around misplacing people. Expressions, so interesting.

I opened my eyes. River had fallen asleep sitting up, head on my lap. Poor puppy. Gently I woke her, then rose from my seat. Spring rain drizzled over the deck.

Memories are good. Heartbreaking, and yet I felt alive, more alive than I had felt in a long time. Perhaps my demons were really imprisoned memories demanding release. Have I chained up my forgiveness as well?

Bone-deep weariness of talking, writing, and thinking about forgiveness sped through me. I should move on. The blog served its purpose, to an extent. Still, I won't take down the blog, as long as there are readers.

One with problem with living in your head is that, when you finally venture out, reality doesn't necessary follow the logic you came up with. Perception is reality, no, not really. Doesn't the Bible show that man cannot alter reality? Grand civilizations were built, nations conquering other nations and, with one word from God, everything crumbled. Men created gods that appealed to their view of reality; God, time and time again, proved mightier than their imagination. Men took God's laws, twisting them into something that oppresses, instead of guides. All to exalt those who hide their sins better than most.

Am I God that I can deny forgiveness?

It all comes back to that, doesn't it?

I opened the door, River entering behind me. She trots to her water bowl while I wander to my chair in the living room. Picking up the book I've been reading—I Forgive You[11] but—I flipped through the pages. A pharisee, with my hard heart. Oh, how easy it is to tear oneself apart.

If I had died that day, would I have opened my eyes at the first resurrection, with the saints or in the second, with the sinners? I have to believe there's a reason I lived. After seeing Jefferson in the woods, rediscovering that bitterness that had hidden so long in my heart, I focused on that. Confronting Jefferson, showing him that letter, giving him the photos—all of that helped and yet didn't help at the same time.

Did I actually say I forgave Jefferson? Do I have that right to do so? Maybe that's the action that's missing.

---

[11] Morales-Gudmundson, Lourdes. *I Forgive You*. Nampa, ID: Pacific Press Publishing Association, 2006.

Vivian's betrayal was tied to Jeremy's death, but he was dying before she had the affair. How could I not see that—well, I did, but how could I not feel that.

With a deep breath, I got up, grabbed my bag and cane, and headed out.

CHAPTER 22

The Fisher Family and Nicole

Until we know another's demons, we cannot presume to fully understand another's choices. We understand, at best, from our knowledge of our personal demons. Even knowing another's struggles, however, does not fully explain the effect on a person's mind. There's heartlessness in laying out one's sin when the offender lies bleeding on the ground.

Why are emotions so messy? Why can't a broken heart become a physical wound that one can heal; why can't physical therapy cure sorrow? My heart was broken; there are no sutures to patch it together. Can I write that another loved less than I because his or her love existed in defiance of another's promise?

I started this blog in my search to forgive. However, in doing so, I found the speck in my own eye, so to speak. I wounded a man who already had been hurt. In exposing his cherished sin, did I free him or trap him?

—ReesesCup76, The Cost of Forgiving Blog

Feeling rather lazy, I jumped into my truck and drove up the split road to Jefferson's cabin—not to stop myself from changing my mind—I knew I needed to at least see Jefferson one last time, though my heart screamed why, what's the point?

For the sake of my conscience?

Human reasoning remains a mystery in some ways, in many ways, for all those who claim predictability.

Several cars filled the small parking area, and I pulled behind Jefferson's vehicle. Hands on wheel, contemplating. Do I go in if he has guests? Nah, this will go faster if there are others around.

With that thought, I exited the truck and made my way up the stairs to the front door. One deep breath and I knocked.

The door swung open. Instead of Jefferson, Nicole stood staring at me, her eyes wide before she crossed her arms.

"What do you want?"

"To be invited in," I replied. She looked better than the last time I had encountered her, more rested.

"No, go away." She started to shut the door.

I fought a snort, stepping forward, "Not your house."

"Who is it, Nikki?"

I stepped back, my amusement fading. I knew that voice. Ellen appeared behind Nicole.

"Reisa. Move aside Nicole," Ellen ordered primly. Nicole scowled at me, but allowed me inside. Seated in the living, Jefferson's sisters and brother Nathan watched me enter. His mother Ginger was in the kitchen, dicing something. She stopped when she saw me.

"Did you move here on purpose to torture him?" Nicole spat.

Had he told her what happened? I stared at Nicole.

"Did you?!" She insisted, suspicion warring with disgust. A scan of the room revealed similar expressions on other people's faces. Ellen alone looked at me with sympathy.

A bitter small laugh escaped my throat.

"I've had enough pain in my life, why on earth would I seek out Jefferson to increase his?"

I noticed the photos then, spend out on the table. Traitorous feet had brought me over, knowing full well what I would see. So easy to avoid, bundled up in a box, here, exposed to the world, I could not look away.

Vivian's bright eyes gleamed at me, her mouth open in midspeech. Sitting on a couch, in an oversized shirt, her surroundings unfamiliar, I wondered why again she had kept this photo. My stomach twisted, my hand reached out to push aside that photo, looking at another it had half-concealed. Jefferson sat on a bench, his arm around Vivian, gazing at her as she smiled at the camera. They must have had a bystander take the photo.

I straightened, running my hand over my face, until I reached my mouth. My throat ached.

"Haven't you seen the photos before? After all, you gave them to Jeff."

I glanced over at Lindsey, I think it is, drawn by the scornful curiosity in her voice. Moving my hand off my mouth to my neck, and massaging the muscles there, I kept my voice as level as possible.

> *I forgot how much I had leaned on her as I navigated being an adult. Jeremy guided me more, but Vivian helped shape the woman.*

"My brother had died and Vivian had killed herself when I found the photos. I didn't exactly dwell on what I found, nor looked though them all. I deliberately ignored their existence."

One photo caught my eye, "Oh, Vivi." I sighed, reaching out, "I didn't know you kept this photo with the others. I assumed…."

My face shined up at me, the girl I once was. Vivian had her arm around me, proudly beaming at the camera. My college graduation. Sorrow caused by my parents' absence overshadowed that day, but Vivian refused to succumb to the depression. All that afternoon she worked to keep Jeremy and I smiling, cracking jokes and teasing. Jeremy, Vivian and I were eight years apart, not far enough for a parental figure, but Vivian managed to invoke a maternal comfort.

I forgot that. I forgot how much I had leaned on her as I navigated being an adult. Jeremy guided me more, but Vivian helped shape the woman. So easy to despise the faults when you forget the virtues, and she had so many….

Tears fought to escape but, in this hostile environment, I feared releasing them. An arm went around me, offering comfort.

"I'm so sorry, honey," Ellen whispered.

I tried to box her in, casting her as a gossip when she hurt me. I should know better, few people have only one face. I turned and buried my head in her shoulder, sobbing.

"Nate, grab some tissues."

Ginger's voice broke through the noise in my head. Lifting my head to give Ellen a watery smile, I sniffed as I stepped back. Nathan stood up, looking around.

"No, thank you. I have some." Reaching into my bag, still hanging on my shoulder, I pulled out a pack of tissues. Deep breath, in and out. I lifted my eyes off the floor, taking in the people silently watching. A joke died on my lips. Nathan gave me a small smile, standing with his hands tucked into the front pockets of his jeans. He opened his mouth to speak but Ellen patted my arm, drawing my attention away.

"I'm sorry." She said, her face ashamed, "Maybe some of what you said was right, I assume much."

"Oh, please." Nicole said but, when I eyed her, Nicole looked away, her cheeks red. She was young, wasn't she?

My mouth twisted, "Well, that was fun." Embarrassed, I turned to the table, Vivian's likeness shattered across my vision.

"Did any of you ever meet her?" I asked.

"No," Ginger replied for the others, "The, err, relationship...." Ginger faltered.

"Vivian didn't want to," Jefferson stood in the hallway entrance. "It was a bone of contention between us. I understood not seeing her family, but my family was different."

"Her family doesn't know about you, as far as I know," I took in Jefferson's haggard face, his hunched shoulders.

"I wouldn't think they did. What are you doing here, Reisa?"

I shrugged, words refusing to arrange themselves properly.

"You wanted to see him suffer," Nicole said, "He is."

Oh, that's it. Nerves raw, I lashed out.

"Suffer?" I repeated. "What changed, really, for him? He didn't know my brother, and he already knew Vivian killed herself. I can see the photos," I glanced at them then at him, "It would renew pain. Why do you think I kept my photos locked up?" I held up my hand as Nicole started to speak, "Not that I assumed anyone wondered. Seriously, Nicole, you are like something out of a bad romance story, the lovely woman spewing hate. The villain the heroine must face. Act like a heroine."

A choking sound, almost like someone fought a laugh, was followed by Ginger's sharp rebuke to Nathan.

"You think I'm not torn up by my part?" Jefferson asked, aghast.

"You didn't force the affair, Jefferson, she had a choice. Besides, it's between you and God, not you and God and me, and Nicole, and your family, and the random person on the street."

For a brief moment, I hesitated. Well, I had shed tears before these people, so why not?

"I spent the last year working on forgiveness, praying for forgetting. I had a realization, never mind the details, but I felt like I needed to see you."

"I knew it," Nicole cried.

My lip curled but I spoke over her. "Anyway, Vivian loved you. She was wrong, you were wrong, but I tied her betrayal to Jeremy's death. I feared I connected the two that way for you. I know I did. I said it sped along Jeremy's death, but I cannot know that, can I? No, his death isn't on you. Whether you knew that already or not, I needed to say it. My actions have been selfish recently," I swallowed thickly. "I didn't mean to burden you or renew your pain. I just wanted to let go." My fist clutched.

"Did it help?" Jefferson said, waving his family and friends silent.

"Yes and no. But when have man's plans ever worked out well for him? God knows the path we should take, over rocky terrain. I'm so very tired of tripping." I laughed, "Oh poor me that sounded so …. I do not even know what I want to say anymore."

I snatched the photo of me and Vivian off the table, "I'm taking this."

Before I could flee through the door, Jefferson stepped in front, "You are trying so hard not to tell me what I am thinking or feeling, nor what I should do. Thank you for that."

Um, okay. I frowned at his back as he disappeared back down the hallway.

"Your brother," Ginger said, coming over to me, "What did he die of?"

Nosey. What does it matter to tell her though?

"He had pancreatic cancer. By the time symptoms appeared, it was too late. He fought anyway. He didn't want to die, until he did," I whispered.

"Oh, honey." Ellen sighed.

"My son did not give him this cancer," Ginger announced.

"Exactly," I met and held her eyes, "No, the cause that led your son and Vivian astray and robbed me of my last living family. Sin. Eve's sin, Adam joining his sin to hers. That's what led to my brother's death."

"Why did you think you had to forgive Jefferson then?" Lindsey interjected.

"Yeah, sounds arrogant, right? What did he do to me, right?" I fought rolling my eyes. "Choices were made, long ago, and choices matter. You can go down a road, but then say, 'Oh, never mind,' and backtrack to the correct path, but the thorny vines that crept behind you, leave wounds in yourself and others. Jeremy would still have died, but I would have had Vivian. I knew her since I was six. She was the only sister I'd ever known. I needed her."

"She chose to kill herself, after betraying her vows."

I winced, and Ginger's face flushed as Ellen mumbled, "Ginger, really!"

"Yes, she did. I felt like dying too after my husband died, add to that guilt…." Deep breath, "Yeah."

"You need to go," Ginger answered. "You are bringing my son pain."

"I'm pretty sure he brought it on himself," Nathan argued, "He's the one who wouldn't leave Reisa here alone. Honestly, he even proposed friendship to her. Isn't it funny, in retrospect, that despite the lengths Reisa went to avoid contact, she's now being blamed for his pain?"

Nathan walked over to his mother and I, his voice furious, "He had an affair with her sister-in-law while her brother was dying. I'm sure she has cause to despise him, instead of how nice she's actually been about the whole mess."

"Nate!" !He ignored her and reached out to squeeze my arm.

"I am so very sorry, Reisa."

Unable to speak, I nodded my acknowledgement before escaping out the door. Behind me I heard voices raised.

CHAPTER 23

Nathan and Nicole

The heart matters. I read the story of Ahab, and it struck me that Ahab believed. He never, that I found, denied Elijah as God's prophet, believing the prophecies.

If Ahab isn't proof that it's not enough to merely believe, look at his ending.

David had many wives, something I hated, honestly, but his sin with Bathsheba was still called adultery. There was forgiveness there, from God. I wonder about Bathsheba, the position she was in. Her king orders her to come to him and, in doing so, she loses her husband. Later, she loses her child. I feel for her, but let's remember that Bathsheba's son took the throne, and she was listed as an ancestor of Jesus. Was that enough to heal her heart?

Off topic as that paragraph appears, it connects to King Ahab. David regretted his sin, and he was punished. For his sins, David repented.

Ahab grieved, humbled himself, but he never changed. His actions cost the lives of so many of God's people. It's easy to see the consequences of Ahab's actions, David's as well, for the Bible records them.

Chapter 23: Nathan and Nicole ✦ 153

Can we stand to read the records of what our sins cost others? Will we think the heart matters then?
—ReesesCup76, The Cost of Forgiving Blog

The blinking curser taunts me, what else shall I say? I reread the words on the screen.

> It's only been a few days, but I have no intention of returning to Jefferson's house or, really, ever seeing him again. If I can help it. I saw this to the end and learned my lesson.
>
> What lesson was that? Well, the one you kept trying to teach me, Selene. I can easily picture your raised brows; you warned me so many times about my active imagination, as Mom did as well. Yes, you acted like my mother at times. You know that's not an insult, right? Friends fill so many roles for each other.
>
> Fine, I'll admit I created impressions of people without knowing them. I even felt as if I knew them, based on what I'd observed about them. Here, this is why I e-mailed, so you have a record; appearances and actions are not all there are to a person. The heart matters.
>
> We..., I judge people by their actions, not their intent, because the ripples on the surface are all that one sees. There are sharks under the surface, though, but also dolphins as well.
>
> Forgive me, my head's aching, can't think straight.

Should I go on? No, Selene will understand if I cannot write more. Typing out a simple good-bye because I need to lay down, I sent the e-mail off. Shielding my eyes from the bright light coming through the window, I shut off the computer.

Why does my head ache so much. I've never had a hangover, but I imagine it's similar to the experience occurring right now. Food makes me nauseous, light bothers me, and my head aches. Stumbling through the house, I end up on the couch, arm over my face.

The pain medicine, of course. The withdrawal symptoms, can't avoid them totally. Of course, brilliant me, I also have the flu. Who can blame my body for hating me. Well, technically, it's my body's fault.

A loud banging came from my head, but also from the front door—just as persistent, too.

"Come on, girl, let's see who it is," I mumbled to River. She lifted her head from her little bed, the only part of her that moved.

"Fine."

Wrapping the throw on the couch around me, I went down the stairs to the door. Not bothering to check who it was—River would feel bad she didn't come with me if I got hurt; no, on second thought, she wouldn't—I opened the door.

Nathan and Nicole stood there, their eyes taking in my disheveled state.

Infusing the word with how pathetic I felt, "Yes?"

One word can express so much.

Nathan stepped forward, while Nicole stepped back. She's a nurse, she was more than aware of how contagious I was. Of course, a <u>good</u> nurse would want to take care of the sick.

I shot a resentful glance her way as Nathan wordlessly guided me up the stairs, over to the couch.

"Nice house, finally get to see it," he said as I stretched out and he managed to unravel me from the throw and place it over me instead. "Where's the kitchen? Never mind, I see it. Nicole," he whispered loudly, a great skill, "shut the door."

The echoes of a slam made me duck my head under the blanket.

"Sheesh, couldn't you be quieter?" I heard Nathan complain. "Hello, girl, want some water?"

I doubted he was asking Nicole. A pang of guilt shot through me for failing to check the pets' water. Write an e-mail? Sure, take care of my pets' basic needs? Nah.

"Here, drink some of this."

Peeking out I saw Nathan standing over me. His concern became edged with amusement as I blinked at him, "Scoot up a bit."

I obliged him, sipping on the ginger ale he brought. "I'm doing better, just hit a wall after finishing some work. Give me a few moments and I can throw you two out."

He ignored the threat.

"How long have you been sick?"

"Sick?" I said in mock outrage, "Do I look sick to you? No, do not answer that." With a wan smile, I sipped some more ginger ale before handing it back to him. He set it on a coaster on the coffee table.

River came over and bumped his leg with her nose. He knelt down, patting her head.

"Hello, River, I've heard about you. Such a pretty girl," he smiled.

I looked past the duo to Nicole, "This a mercy mission?"

"It is now," Nathan gave River one last pat, getting back up. "Nicole came to apologize for her behavior."

Nicole averted her eyes. She really was like a little girl, even having someone force her to apologize.

I stared at her, then Nathan, "Really? For what?"

"My behavior at Jeff's and, um, other times," Nicole crossed her arms. "So sorry."

"Accepted. Good-bye." I slid down.

"Really Cole? You can't do better than that?" Nathan sounded exasperated.

"What? I am sorry. But I still do not trust her."

"You didn't trust me before this came out," I rasped, my throats aching, "Seriously, this whole thing's so ridiculous. I've had people dislike me, even hate me, but accuse me of even half the stuff you have…"

"Like what?" Nathan interjected.

Ignoring his question I continued, "I have absolutely no problem staying away from you, but I'm not about to bend over backwards to do it."

I reached for the ginger ale, Nathan grabbing it first to hand it to me.

"I should not have brought her with me."

"Nathan," Nicole protested. Why I do not know.

"Okay, why are you here? Going to say sorry, too?"

"For what?" Nathan ran his hand through his hair, ruffling it up. "I can try to apologize for my family's behavior but…."

He shrugged.

"I'm leaving," Nicole declared, stomping down the stairs then out the door. Both Nathan and I winced as she slammed the door.

"Hope she wasn't your ride."

"She wasn't," he assumed me, his eye twinkling. "Don't worry, you aren't stuck with me. Even if she was, I'm staying at Jefferson's and the weather's nice for a walk."

Silence fell, then Nathan sat down on the floor next to the couch. River immediately plopped down next to him, and he stoked her fur, his eyes distant.

"I wanted to share something with you," he held up his hand to still my protest, "Hear me out, please. Jefferson struggles with alcohol. He has since he was twenty-three. Drugs as well, at one point, but alcohol appears to have the firmer grip."

I closed my eyes, leaning my head back.

He went on.

"Not many people know, but he almost trashed his career over the years. Nicole, from what I gather, wants to save him."

"An idealistic dreamer," I commented with scorn.

"True. She can't seem to understand you can't force the love she wants from him. Ellen admits she shouldn't have exposed Cole to so many unrealistic love stories. At one point, those was all Cole read."

"Some people have no trouble separating the fantasy from reality," I reminded him.

"Again, true. Some people can't." He must have felt the words I refused to say, for he added, "Becoming a nurse should have brought realism into her life. If she had chosen a job that exposed her to drug addicts and users…, but she didn't. She works with her cousin's friend's uncle," Nathan chuckled, "Small town, remember? The fact you settled in so well, maintained your distance so thoroughly, yet stayed well-liked baffles some of us."

"Nice to know some people like me," I twisted my mouth into a smile. "Jefferson, our talk sent him down into the bottle, so to speak." I turned on my side to see Nathan's face.

"No. Quite the opposite. I have my theories on why as well. Jefferson idolized Vivian, which became easier with time erasing her flaws. He felt guilt that he couldn't save her, he thought." Nathan ran his hand through his hair again. "He should tell you this, but I'm thinking he needs to leave you alone. With you telling him the truth of what occurred, that idol shattered."

"Well, if we are going to discuss this…." I sighed, I wanted done. Done with all of this. Moving my gaze away from him, I stared straight ahead.

"Jefferson had another guilt to battle, when his cherished sin was exposed, I'm guessing, of course. Vivian was a flawed, sweet, weak woman. I loved her, and whereas Jefferson idolized her, I demonized her. Who was more wrong?" I smiled, "Who's to say? When the two opposite met, we humanize Vivian."

"Is that enough to forgive her?"

My gaze jerked back to him.

"Why do you care?"

Nathan looked uncomfortable, "I'm nosy? No, more than curious, I wondered because, if…."

"Yes," I answered, stopping his floundering, "Steadily, each day, I'm forgiving."

Nathan searched my face, "Jefferson claimed he saw you and he felt something wake up. Something that had died with Vivian. Personally, I thought he was romanticizing based on what Ellen told us. A lonely pretty woman…."

I felt the flush in my cheeks, but not from embarrassment. Annoyed, I still cracked a joke.

"You left out *young*."

Nathan laughed, "Youngish woman. Still pretty, if past her first bloom."

I snorted a laugh.

"Slightly sensitive about her age." Nathan sobered, "You brought Jefferson back from his dark place and then delivered a punch that should have knocked him back."

"I should plead ignorance," I muttered, "which is true. Truth is harsh; I'm not sure it would have changed my path."

"It shouldn't." Nathan, moving closer to me, stated. "I love my brother, but he's lived a selfish life of late. His pursuit of you, who wanted solitude, shows how selfish he had become. Now, as for your confrontation, Jefferson went not to the bottle, but to his Bible. He likened himself to Jacob, only to find himself David instead."

Lip quirking up, I complimented him, "Nice."

"Thank you. I read your blog, you know. I've picked up on some of your methods of thought." Nathan's joking grin ease the creepiness. "I'm studying for the ministry as well. Learning to insert those biblical references."

My voice softened as I told him, "My father was a minister."

Nathan patted my hand as I blinked tears.

"Being sick makes one emotional," I reasoned.

"Sorry," Nathan withdrew his hand, looking down at River instead. "Still, I needed to say these things."

"Any more left?"

"With Jefferson, he used to pride himself on his treatment of women. In the past, I've been subjected to his lectures," Nathan gave a sheepish look. "Funny how they came after what happened. He struggled with addiction, that's his weakness, not lust."

"I know he loved Vivian. That neither adds nor subtracts pain for me. Borrowing your expression, funny how I went back and forth on whether I needed to forgive her."

Nathan lifted his eyes to mine. I noticed they were more blue than gray, his face more squarish than his brother's. More glints of red showed up in his hair. Young, so young.

"How old are you?"

"How old are you?" he returned playfully.

"Thirty-nine."

Startled that I answered him, he replied, "Twenty-eight. I came to the ministry late."

"Jefferson's what, thirty-three?"

"Yep."

Tired, I flatted out on my back. "So young."

Nathan got up, "Cause you are so much older." He placed his cool hand on my forehead. "You're burning up."

"Yeah."

Like a flick of a switch, my eyes grew heavy.

"Why don't you get some sleep," Nathan said as I drifted off.

CHAPTER 24

Nathan

I met a man who thought his lover was in a bad marriage. He learned, to his shame, she was the bad part of the marriage.

Adultery is never the answer.

Christ said that, for the hardening of their hearts, Moses allowed divorce. In God's eyes, divorce is permissible only when there's infidelity. Permissible, not required.

Forgiving someone for their cheating, their sin, a difficult task, is the right thing. Our God knows our hearts; He knows the pain betrayal wretches. We can walk away.

Some people forgive, and their spouses do not stop.

There are those who condemn spouses who give up. Isn't that interesting? How can you tell another person how much his or her heart can take?

Only God knows.

How hard it is for humans to bear the iniquities of others. We cannot see the heart, and forgiving is so very hard when you don't understand the motives.

In my search for quotes on forgiveness, I found this:

> *Until we have seen someone's darkness, we don't really know who they are. Until we have forgiven someone's darkness, we do not really know what love is.*[12]
>
> It begs the question, whose darkness have I seen and still forgave them?
>
> I loved a man once. When he exposed his darkness, when he hurt me, I turned away.
>
> It's not enough to believe, you must act. It's not enough to love, you must forgive.
>
> The relief that comes with knowing that finally, this, this I can do. I can let go. Yet, with one ghost slowly vanishing, I'm left alone. Bitterness was a friend that kept despair away.
>
> —ReesesCup76, The Cost of Forgiving Blog

"So, Jefferson's alright?"

Nathan jumped slightly, turning to me. He had stood in the hallway, looking over my photos for at least ten minutes. That's how long I'd been watching him. He headed over to me.

"Yes, he is. In fact, he left on assignment. I'm watching the house."

"Oh, sweetie, aren't you supposed to be in school?" I joked.

"No." He sat down on the ground, "Let's discuss something else, Tell me about your husband."

"Yeah. No." Trying to sit up, my head felt fuzzy. I laid down.

"Sorry, too personal."

"Very much so. The other things we've discussed, I can see that, but, yeah, too personal."

"Your injuries then, that cannot be personal, right?"

With a chuckle in answer to the smile on his face, I informed him.

"I'm weaning myself off my pain meds; you might want to remember how unpredictable addicts are."

"What have you been taking?"

I told him and his whistled, "Heavy stuff."

"You are familiar with drugs, not a good sign."

---

[12] "Marianne Williamson Quotable Quote." Goodreads. https://1ref.us/1su. Accessed December 31, 2021.

"I went to medical school. Loma Linda, then John Hopkins."

"Lots of money," I responded.

"True. I liked Maryland, not as much as my fiancée did though. She's still there, and not my fiancée anymore." His grin flashed, "There, that's personal."

"Oh?"

"It wasn't tragic, just grew apart, wanted different things."

"Slow death," I commented, bending my arms to tuck them front of me.

"Yeah. So slow, you do not notice the bleeding until the life has already left."

"Sad," I said, "but I'm stealing that."

Nathan shook his head, his lips upturned. "I've read your stories. Both online and book form. I liked them. They were sad."

"Ever notice how many classics are sad? We understand sorrow better than joy, for the most part. I understand sorrow better, but I'm not always sad."

Nathan nodded, looking unconvinced, before drawing a deep breath.

"My brother is no David. I said that, but, no."

"Alright."

"Not that he's not good, just…." He stopped, trying to reason it out.

"How complex David was, yet his heart, well, heart matters. I'm not going to judge, not anymore." I paused, "My injuries."

Relief flashed across his face before he frowned, "Jefferson told me a rock slide."

"My left leg was pinned under a rock for two hours. I almost lost it. A serious compound break in the femur, compartment syndrome," I paused, "Throwing out terms here. Surgeries, scars….Why I do not wear shorts. There's pain and, of course, a limp."

"How long ago?"

"Three years. I would have died if Elijah haven't shielded me. It's amazing how he didn't crush me."

"Jeff said you do not remember much."

"Jefferson shares a lot on about people," I commented, "but yeah, that's the lovely part about digging into your past memories. It unearths more than you want."

Nathan bowed his head, "Tragedy, the fabric of life."

"There's no one thread in that fabric," I corrected, "Forgiveness, atonement, salvation, and hope are all woven in. Especially hope."

"Job's wife told him to curse God and die, although some version have her saying 'bless.'"

"I'm not Job. Simply Reisa, living the life I've pieced together."

Nathan smiled.

I shifted, sitting up. My head protested weakly, but I managed to stay upright.

Nathan jumped up, "When's the last time you ate?"

"I do not know. I forgot to check the pets' water and food. Sebastian?"

I heard a chirp, and then Sebastian came padding out of my office.

"I'll feed him as well. Where's the food."

"In the lower cabinet to the right of the sink. It pulls out. Thank you."

Sebastian jumped up, curling in my lap. The affection lasted until he heard his food being poured. He abandoned me for the kitchen.

"Beautiful kitty."

"Thank you, he's a Maine Coon." I maneuver myself so my back was against the back of the couch.

"I never saw one with silver fur," Nathan came over, standing to the side of the couch. "Do you have any soup? Or ingredients? Never mind, I'll go check."

Nathan disappeared back into my kitchen.

"You are pushy, you know."

"Yeah, but it's for a good cause." He peeked around the wall at me, "You need someone currently, and your pets can't cook." His head disappeared again.

Too sick to protest, I leaned forward and grabbed a book off the coffee table.

"I do not even know you," I informed him.

"You do. You knew I studied to be a doctor, am studying to be a minster instead. I had a fiancée at one point, who still lives in Maryland. I pulled a Jonah, I've been a bit of a cad in the past, and you have even met my family."

"And you like taking care of sick people."

"Exactly. See? We are friends."

Sebastian, tummy satisfied, returned. He purred as I absentmindedly stroked his fur. Pride, for me, goes out the window when I'm sick. I read while Nathan cooked.

Chapter 24: Nathan

"Do you have a tray?"

"On top of the fridge."

With measured steps, Nathan brought the steaming bowl over to me. "I found your stash of frozen soup."

"Thank you," I put the book down as Nathan shooed my kitty away. Tray in my lap, I breathed in the aroma, "Minestrone."

Nathan went to the kitchen and returned with his own bowl. Throwing a place mat on the coffee table, he sat next to it. "Hope you do not mind, but this is the tax on my cooking."

I closed my eyes, saying a brief blessing, and opened my eyes to observe Nathan doing the same.

We ate in silence for a few minutes.

"Your animals are well trained. They are leaving the food alone."

"It's River's naptime, and Sebastian hates human food. Outside of fish, I'm told. I do not eat fish, which solves any issues."

Nathan nodded, spooning his soup into his mouth.

"What's next for your leg? The amount of pain I've witnessed, are they able to do anything?"

"As I said, along with the damage to my leg, other issues have developed. Infections muscle damage, the like. They have attempted to repair the damage, but last surgery I had, I almost died from an infection afterwards. At this point, I'm calling it the thorn in my flesh."

Nathan dropped his spoon into the empty bowl, "Giving up."

"Accepting. Even if they manage to 'fix'—I used quotation marks, spoon in hand—"my leg, it will never be the same."

"Therefore the constant remainder."

"Of Elijah's death? It's not the only remainder. The empty bed, the silence, the absence of tender touch," I swallowed, laying my spoon down. "I had wonderful years with him, too short, any amount would have been."

"No children?"

"Elijah," I stopped, bursting out in laughter, "you've got me talking about him. Clever."

Nathan stood up, "Finished?"

"Yes, thank you."

Nathan added his bowl to the tray, whisking it away. I heard the faucet, then the dishwasher open and shut. He reappeared, informing, "I'll take care of the pot and soup remaining once it all cools down."

"Thank you."

"No problem. I didn't even think, do you need to take something?"

I shook my head, wrapping the throw around me, "No. Rest is most important. Could you let River outside? I use the back door."

"Of course. Wake up girl, time to go potty."

River stood up, stretching with a wide yawn before following Nathan to the back door. Such a smart dog.

Sebastian returned to me, forgiving me for eating, already asleep in my lap when the duo returned. Nathan must have walked River instead of releasing her in the yard. They were gone a good thirty minutes. Nathan went to the kitchen as River drank, the noise of the faucet informing what he was up to.

"I need to go," Nathan said when he emerged from the kitchen, "I'll check on you later. I, like a stalker, have your phone number. I can pick up whatever you need from the store and swing it by tomorrow. Can I get you anything before I go?"

"My phone and laptop."

"Let's get you into bed, then I will bring those to you."

Scooping Sebastian up in my arms, I stood up, wobbling slightly. Nathan reached out but I shook my head.

"I've been getting around alright. I guess I hit a wall when you showed up, but I'm getting better."

"Right," Nathan didn't sound convinced. "While you are still quite pretty, you look half-dead."

Nathan followed me into the bedroom, rushing around me to pull back the covers of the bed. "Where are your things?"

"Laptop and phone are both in my office."

Sebastian tolerated me crawling into bed with him. Nathan pulled the covers over us, which Sebastian actually appear to like.

"Alright, I noticed the office earlier."

I sank into the cool sheets, closing my eyes.

"I'll put this next to you, within reach." I heard Nathan say.

Opening my eyes, I observed him studying my wedding portrait.

"I brought Nicole over to have her apologize and to tell you about Jefferson. I wondered, in the back of my mind, if you wanted revenge. Jefferson's right, a few minutes in your presence, and it's hard to believe bad of you." Nathan turned to me, meeting my eyes, "You have this allure around you, basic goodness."

I laughed.

Chapter 24: Nathan

"And humility. Aren't you tired of other people telling you what you are? I am, but I'm heading into a calling that requires political skills at times. You are hiding."

"I have nine years on you, nine more years of living among people, of realizing that not everyone is called to act the extrovert. There's more than one way to witness."

"You witness through your stories."

"I try." I closed my eyes, "Christ calls us to go into all nations, sometimes words can reach where people can't. Where people reject the idea of reading biblical texts…."

"You mix them in. Conceal them."

"I list my stories as Christian."

"C.S. Lewis viewed his Narnia series as Christian, yet there are still those who do not connect the people and themes to the Bible."

"I'm not hiding," I told him, addressing his earlier comment.

"No, I misspoke." Nathan's attention returned to the photo, "If your husband was alive, what would you be doing."

"We lived in a restored farmhouse in western Maryland. Elijah worked from home, like me. We had a tiny group of friends, attended a decent-sized church, and we preferred camping to socializing. If he was still alive, I would still be a homebody."

"But you wouldn't be alone."

"No." I breathed, "No. I wouldn't be alone."

"You're not alone," Nathan walked to the door, pausing in the doorway to look back at me. "You draw people to you, you know. I personally find you fascinating."

"It's my mystique."

Nathan chuckled, "The mystery appeals, but I found you interesting before I even met you. I have followed "The Introvert Review" for years. I remember when someone took over for a period, due to you being unavailable…."

"Friends filled in."

"I've read your stories. I'm rather interested in knowing you. Thankfully, I'll have time."

"Oh."

"I graduated, this church is among my new post." He turned to me.

I closed my eyes, "Oh, goody."

I heard Nathan chuckle as his steps faded down the hallway.

CHAPTER 25

Forgiveness

I struggled with forgiveness, with forgetting. To my relief, no matter how painful that confrontation was, no matter how much I doubted the wisdom of it, God used it to heal two souls.

I've forgiven Vivian, my sister-in-law, for her betrayal, and I have forgotten her lover as well. I won't even go into how arrogant I feel writing that or my uncertainty concerning whether the crime was mine to forgive. I held a grudge, which would have trapped my soul.

What's left for me? Jeremy's still gone, and Elijah, my heart mate, is as well. Elijah didn't want to survive without me, his actions left me here without him. When we meet in heaven, I'm pointing that out to him.

I struggled to forgive. Letting go of that anger revealed the grief beneath. God used Elijah's death to help me make peace.

It's done, so where do I go from here? I didn't move to this place to find Vivian's lover (still not giving his name, sorry), but his existence in this place overrode, emotionally, all my other issues.

I'm alone. I have elected to remain so, outside of friendship. I do not desire to marry again. Some can find another love, one different from the one they lost. I do not know if I would ever want to. Moving on, I can't. No one else will ever suit me like Elijah.

Alone, I'm content. Why look for another spouse when my memories keep me warm? The times in Elijah's arms, the roaring laugh, the crinkles around his eyes.

The pain's bittersweet. I've loved and been loved. With the freedom of forgiveness, I have no more bonds holding me from salvation.

TEACH Services, Inc.
P U B L I S H I N G
www.TEACHServices.com • (800) 367-1844

We invite you to view the complete
selection of titles we publish at:
www.TEACHServices.com

We encourage you to write us
with your thoughts about this,
or any other book we publish at:
info@TEACHServices.com

TEACH Services' titles may be purchased in
bulk quantities for educational, fund-raising,
business, or promotional use.
bulksales@TEACHServices.com

Finally, if you are interested in seeing
your own book in print, please contact us at:
publishing@TEACHServices.com
We are happy to review your manuscript at no charge.

www.ingramcontent.com/pod-product-compliance
Lightning Source LLC
Chambersburg PA
CBHW070553160426
43199CB00014B/2491